Turtle Soup

Recipes for the Specific Carbohydrate Diet™ from an SCD Mom

Published by:

Beth Spencer Fine Arts
Muskegon, MI

ISBN 978-1-257-97798-7

Library of Congress Control Number: 2011914861

Specific Carbohydrate Diet and SCD are trademarks of Kirkton Press and are used with permission.

To order additional copies of *Turtle Soup* please visit:

www.lulu.com

or

www.beth-spencer.com

For Amy

Eat well - Be well

thank you

To Elaine Gottschall B.A., M.Sc., for her revolutionary work in the field of irritable bowel syndrome (IBS) and irritable bowel disease (IBD), documented in her book, *Breaking the Vicious Cycle: Intestinal Health through Diet*, providing relief for many who suffer with IBS and IBD; a grain-free, gluten-free, refined-sugar-free, low-lactose plan, based in sound nutrition; the Specific Carbohydrate Diet™ (SCD).

To Judy Herrod, Elaine Gottschall's daughter, who graciously read my manuscript and helped me fine-tune the recipes, making certain that all the ingredients are 100% "legal,"* and then granting me permission to use the term: Specific Carbohydrate Diet™.

To Julie Rabbitt, who recommended the SCD and pointed my daughter in the direction of what I hope is a lifetime of intestinal health.

To Raman Prasad and Lucy Rosset, who read the manuscript and gave me great feedback.

To Megan Trank, who edited the manuscript.

To Sara Spencer, my lovely graphic designing daughter, for helping with the cover.

To Amy McKenna, my other lovely daughter. It was so much fun working together, inventing tummy-friendly treats for your sweet tooth, as well as savory adaptations of family favorites using SCD "legal"* ingredients.

*For a list of legal and illegal foods for the Specific Carbohydrate Diet™, see:
Breaking the Vicious Cycle: Intestinal Health through Diet, p.p.73-8, or visit:
http://www.breakingtheviciouscycle.info/legal/legal_illegal_a-c.htm

about turtle soup

In 1995, my daughter was diagnosed with **Crohn's** disease. It all began when Amy was a junior in high school. She developed a fistula, which after repair and biopsy revealed **Crohn's** type tissue. Her gastroenterologist warned that she would need to keep an eye out for the disease to worsen, possibly years down the road. For the time being, watchful waiting was all we could do.

Five years later, sure enough, Amy was in severe, chronic pain; a colonoscopy revealed **Crohn's** lesions in the small bowel. Placed on medications with scary sounding side effects and told to eat whatever she wanted, since there was no known dietary solution—Amy faced a lifetime of medication, and in the worst-case scenario, multiple surgeries. Fortunately, Amy went into remission, enabling her to get off medication long enough to have her first child. But several months after her healthy baby girl was born, Amy's symptoms returned with a vengeance—and she went back on medication. But this time, her symptoms did not respond as well as they had the first time.

When Amy and her husband began thinking about having a second child, they got conflicting advice from several doctors about the safety of continuing medication while pregnant. Amy definitely did not want to risk exposing her unborn baby to medications with unknown side effects, but she also didn't want to have a **Crohn's** flare-up during pregnancy.

My friend Julie has lived with **Crohn's** for over twenty years and has five children. I knew that she followed a special diet to control her symptoms and that she'd been mostly medication-free for years. Amy was desperate enough to try almost anything. So I called Julie and poured out my heart. She told me about Elaine Gottschall's ***Breaking the Vicious Cycle: Intestinal Health Through Diet***, a book detailing the **Specific Carbohydrate Diet™ (SCD)** and about the great success she's had with it. Julie graciously agreed to call Amy.

Within the week, Amy had begun the first stage of the diet; within the month, she began weaning off her medication; and within two months she was happily and healthily pregnant—feeling better than ever. For moral support, I joined Amy on the diet and together we learned how to bake with new ingredients, planning meals and revising family favorite recipes following the **SCD's** grain-free, gluten-free, refined-sugar-free, low-lactose guidelines.

Best of all, after a healthy pregnancy, Amy gave birth to a thriving baby girl. And when she went to her gastroenterologist for her check-up, her doctor commended her progress—although unable to officially credit the **SCD**, he told her to keep doing what she was doing. It's been four medication-free years since Amy started the **SCD**—and she continues to feel great!

The **turtle**, slow and steady, hard-shelled and sturdy, is an ancient symbol for health and longevity—and **soup** represents everything that is warm and healing and restorative—I hope you enjoy cooking and eating the delicious recipes in ***Turtle Soup*** as much as Amy and I did creating them. May you find a way of health, happiness, and peace-of-gut.

bon appétit!

to the reader:

The recipes in **Turtle Soup**, when used in conjunction with Elaine Gottschall's book, *Breaking the Vicious Cycle: Intestinal Health through Diet* (BTVC), may help certain individuals with IBS and other bowel diseases such as ulcerative colitis, Crohn's disease, and celiac disease that has not responded to gluten-free diets.

The author recommends that the reader refer to BTVC, and/or www.breakingtheviciouscycle.info as the primary resource for the Specific Carbohydrate Diet™. However, readers should not attempt self-diagnosis or self-treatment, nor should they use **Turtle Soup** or BTVC as a substitute for advice from a qualified health professional.

The naming of any product does not constitute an endorsement, nor is compensation received by the author. The case histories contained in this book are anecdotal and only true for the time period about which this book was written.

table of contents:

bon appétit!

banana muffins
Makes 12

2 large eggs, well-beaten
⅓ cup honey
4 T. unsalted butter, melted
1 ripe banana, mashed
¾ tsp. baking soda
½ tsp. salt
¼ tsp. ground nutmeg
1 tsp. SCD "legal" vanilla extract (*no added sugars*)
2½ cups blanched almond flour
½ cup chopped pecans or walnuts

Preheat the oven to 325° F. Line a muffin pan with paper liners.

In a large bowl, whisk together the beaten eggs, honey, and melted butter. Stir in the mashed banana, baking soda, salt, nutmeg, vanilla, and almond flour until well-combined. Fold in the chopped nuts.

Divide the batter between the muffin cups, using wet fingers to lightly press down any large bumps on the top of the batter.

Bake the muffins for 20-25 minutes, until nicely browned, springy to the touch, and a toothpick inserted in the center of a muffin comes out clean. Cool the muffins 10 minutes in the pan, then transfer them to a wire rack to finish cooling.

Muffins will keep in an airtight container at room temperature for up to a week. They also freeze well.

carrot muffins
Makes 12

3 large eggs, well-beaten
½ cup honey
¼ cup (½ stick) unsalted butter, melted
½ tsp. baking soda
½ tsp. salt
½ tsp. SCD "legal" vanilla extract (*no added sugars*)
1 tsp. ground cinnamon
2½ cups blanched almond flour
½ cup grated carrot *(Squeeze out as much moisture as possible between paper towels.)*
½ cup white raisins
½ cup chopped walnuts

Preheat the oven to 325° F. Line a muffin pan with paper liners.

In a large bowl, whisk together the beaten eggs, honey, melted butter, baking soda, salt, vanilla, and cinnamon. Stir in the almond flour until well-combined. Fold in the carrots, raisins, and walnuts.

Divide the batter between the muffin cups, using wet fingers to lightly press down any large bumps on the top of the batter.

Bake the muffins for 20-25 minutes, until nicely browned, springy to the touch, and a toothpick inserted in the center of a muffin comes out clean. Cool the muffins 10 minutes in the pan, then transfer them to a wire rack to finish cooling.

Muffins will keep in an airtight container at room temperature for up to a week. They also freeze well.

lemon poppy seed muffins - Amy McKenna
Makes 12

3 large eggs, well-beaten
½ cup honey
¼ cup (½ stick) unsalted butter, melted
½ tsp. baking soda
¼ tsp. salt
1 T. fresh lemon juice
1 T. grated lemon rind *(from the fresh lemon)*
1 T. poppy seeds*
3 cups blanched almond flour

Preheat the oven to 325° F. Line a muffin pan with paper liners.

In a large bowl, whisk together the beaten eggs, honey, melted butter, baking soda, salt, lemon juice, lemon rind, and poppy seeds*. Stir in the almond flour until well-combined.

Divide the batter between the muffin cups, using wet fingers to lightly press down any large bumps on the top of the batter.

Bake the muffins for 25-30 minutes, until nicely browned, springy to the touch, and a toothpick inserted in the center of a muffin comes out clean. Cool the muffins 10 minutes in the pan, then transfer them to a wire rack to finish cooling.

Muffins will keep in an airtight container at room temperature for up to a week. They also freeze well.

*Seeds should not be consumed until symptom-free for 3 months.

peanut butter muffins
Makes 12-16

1 cup natural *(100% peanut)* peanut butter
½ cup honey
3 large eggs, well-beaten
½ tsp. baking soda
½ tsp. salt
¼ cup neutral tasting vegetable oil *(I use grape seed or sunflower oil.)*
2 T. SCD "legal" yogurt *(See instructions, page 68.)*
2 cups blanched almond flour

Preheat the oven to 325° F. Line a muffin pan with paper liners.

Beat together the peanut butter and honey.

Add the beaten eggs, baking soda, salt, oil, and yogurt and beat well.

Mix in the almond flour and stir until well-combined.

Fill the muffin cups almost-full for 12 large muffins, ¾-full for 14-16 medium muffins.

Bake the muffins 20-25 minutes for large muffins, 15-20 minutes for medium muffins, until nicely browned, springy to the touch, and a toothpick inserted in the center of a muffin comes out clean. Cool the muffins 10 minutes in the pan, then transfer them to a wire rack to finish cooling.

Muffins will keep in an airtight container at room temperature for up to a week. They also freeze well.

pumpkin muffins
Makes 12

2 large eggs, well-beaten
½ cup Fresh Pumpkin Purée *(See recipe below.)*
⅓ cup honey
¼ cup (½ stick) unsalted butter, melted
1 tsp. SCD "legal" vanilla extract *(no added sugars)*
¾ tsp. baking soda
½ tsp. salt
1½ tsp. ground cinnamon
½ tsp. ground nutmeg
¼ tsp. ground cloves
¼ tsp. ground ginger
2½ cups blanched almond flour
½ cup chopped walnuts
½ cup raisins

Preheat the oven to 325° F. Line a muffin pan with paper liners.

In a large bowl, combine all ingredients *except* the almond flour, walnuts, and raisins. Stir in the almond flour until well-combined. Fold in the walnuts and raisins. Divide the batter between the muffin cups, using wet fingers to lightly press down any large bumps on the top of the batter. Bake the muffins for 25-30 minutes, until nicely browned, springy to the touch, and a toothpick inserted in the center of a muffin comes out clean. Cool the muffins 10 minutes in the pan, then transfer them to a wire rack to finish cooling. Muffins will keep in an airtight container at room temperature for up to a week. They also freeze well.

Fresh Pumpkin Purée: Preheat the oven to 400° F. Halve 2 small "pie pumpkins" *(available in autumn in larger grocery stores)*. Remove the seeds and strings. Place the pumpkins cut-side-down on a large, rimmed baking pan. Pour enough water in the pan to *just* cover the bottom of the pan. Cover the pan with another sheet of foil and seal the edges of the foil completely. Poke a couple holes in the foil to vent it. Bake the pumpkins for 45-60 minutes until fork-tender. *(I poke a sharp fork right through the foil to test for doneness.)* Remove the pan to a cooling rack. Carefully open one corner of the foil to let the steam escape. Let the pumpkins stand until cool enough to handle. Scrape the flesh away from the skin and place the flesh in a food processor. Purée it until smooth. Transfer the purée to a colander or sieve that has been lined with a coffee filter or cheesecloth and set it atop a large bowl. Refrigerate the bowl and let the purée drip for several hours or overnight. Discard liquid. Freeze leftover purée for later use.

caramel pecan coffee cake
Serves 12

For the topping:
    ½ cup (1 stick) butter
    ½ cup honey
    ¾ cup chopped pecans

Spice mixture:
    ½ cup blanched almond flour
    1 tsp. ground cinnamon

For the dough:
    3 large eggs, well-beaten
    ¼ cup honey
    ¼ cup (½ stick) unsalted butter, melted
    ¼ tsp. apple cider vinegar
    ½ tsp. baking soda
    ¼ tsp. salt
    3 cups blanched almond flour

Generously butter a 9" round cake pan and line the bottom with parchment paper. To make the topping, melt ½ cup butter and ½ cup honey together in a small saucepan. Bring the mixture to a boil and cook for 5 minutes. Pour the caramel into the cake pan. Scatter the pecans over the caramel. Set the cake pan aside.

In a small bowl, combine the ingredients for the spice mixture and set aside.

In a medium bowl, whisk together the beaten eggs, honey, melted butter, vinegar, baking soda, and salt. Stir in the almond flour until well-combined. Wet your hands a little; roll a heaping tablespoon of dough into a ball between your palms. Roll the dough ball in the spice mixture to coat it evenly. Place the dough ball in the cake pan on top of the caramel. Repeat with the rest of the dough, arranging the coated dough balls close together—you will end up with about 12. Flatten the tops of the dough balls a bit with moistened fingers when they are all arranged in the pan.

Bake at 325° F. for 30 minutes or until a toothpick inserted near the center comes out clean and the center seems firm. Loosen the edges with a table knife and invert the cake *immediately* onto a serving plate. Let the cake cool to room temperature and serve. The cake may be stored in an airtight container at room temperature for up to a week. It freezes well.

cashew pancakes - (dairy free)

Makes 10-12

1 cup raw cashews
3 large eggs
2 T. water
¼ tsp. apple cider vinegar
1 T. honey*
1 tsp. cinnamon*
¼ tsp. SCD "legal" vanilla extract (*no added sugars*)
¼ tsp. salt
½ tsp. baking soda
vegetable oil for the griddle
additional honey, warmed

In the work bowl of a food processor, grind the cashews *just* until they begin to clump together and form paste-like globules. Scrape the bottom and sides of the food processor and add the rest of the ingredients to the work bowl. Process the mixture until very smooth. Transfer the batter to a small bowl. If the batter seems too thick, add a little more water. The batter should be the consistency of normal pancake batter.

Generously oil a non-stick griddle (or a large skillet) and heat it on medium-low. Pour a scant ¼ cup of batter onto the griddle for each pancake. Cook the pancakes for about 3 minutes until they firm up and are nicely browned on the bottom. With an oiled spatula, carefully flip the pancakes and cook the other side.

Serve with warmed honey.

*If you want to make savory pancakes, omit the honey and cinnamon.
Add ½ tsp. herbs of your choice. They make excellent flatbreads for sandwiches.

cinnamon walnut scones

Makes about 12

3 large eggs, well-beaten
¼ cup honey
¼ cup (½ stick) unsalted butter, melted
½ tsp. salt
½ tsp. baking soda
1 tsp. ground cinnamon
¼ tsp. apple cider vinegar
2¾ cups blanched almond flour
½ cup currants or raisins
½ cup chopped walnuts

Preheat the oven to 325° F.

In a large bowl, whisk together the beaten eggs, honey, and melted butter. Add the salt, baking soda, cinnamon, and vinegar and mix well. Stir in the almond flour, currants, and nuts to make a fairly stiff dough.

Drop by heaping tablespoons on a baking stone or on a cookie sheet that has been lined with parchment paper.

Flatten each scone a little with a silicone spatula or wet fingers.

Bake the scones 25-30 minutes until nicely browned, firm when inserted with a toothpick, and hollow sounding when tapped.

Cool the scones on a wire rack. Scones keep well in an airtight container at room temperature for at least a week. They freeze well.

mini donuts

Makes about 20 small donuts—12 if using a donut pan

3 large eggs, well-beaten
⅓ cup honey
¼ cup (½ stick) unsalted butter, melted
¼ tsp. apple cider vinegar
¼ tsp. salt
½ tsp. baking soda
1½ tsp. ground nutmeg
2½-3 cups blanched almond flour

Preheat the oven to 325° F.

In a medium bowl, whisk together the beaten eggs, honey, melted butter, vinegar, salt, baking soda, and nutmeg. Stir in the almond flour to make a stiff dough that holds its shape.

Transfer half the dough to a pastry bags that has been fitted with a 1/2" round tip.

Line a cookie sheet with parchment paper. Pipe small donut shapes onto the parchment paper, refilling the pastry bag as needed.

Bake the donuts for 15-20 minutes until golden-brown and firm to the touch. Cool them on a wire rack.

They also bake nicely in a well-buttered, non-stick donut pan. Fill the molds level with the top of the pan, patting the dough down a bit with wet fingers. Bake for 20-25 minutes. Let the donuts cool about 15 minutes before removing them carefully from the pan. If they stick, use a small spatula to loosen them at the edges. Cool the donuts on a wire rack.

These keep well in an airtight container at room temperature for up to a week. They also freeze well.

sausage*

Makes about 12 patties

1 lb. ground pork
1 tsp. dried sage
½ tsp. dried marjoram
¼ tsp. paprika
1 tsp. salt
¾ tsp. black pepper
a pinch of nutmeg
a pinch of allspice
a pinch of cayenne pepper

In a large bowl, mix all ingredients with a fork until well-combined.

With dampened fingers, shape the sausage into small patties.

Generously coat a large skillet with olive oil. Heat the pan on medium to medium-high until the surface of the oil begins to shimmer.

Place the sausage patties in batches in the hot oil. Cook them for 5 minutes on one side, then flip them over and cook them for 5 minutes on the other side.

Drain the sausage patties on paper towels.

*For "Pizza," page 43, cook the sausage mixture, breaking it up as is cooks, until browned, about 10 minutes. Drain the cooked sausage on paper towels.

sunflower walnut bread

Makes 1 loaf
This bread makes a fantastic grilled cheese sandwich.

1 cup walnuts
¼ cup raw sunflower seeds*
3 large eggs
⅓ cup neutral tasting vegetable oil *(I use grape seed oil.)*
1 tsp. honey
½ tsp. salt
1 tsp. baking soda
4 cups blanched almond flour

Preheat the oven to 300° F.

Line a bread pan with parchment paper. *(Tear off a piece of paper big enough to allow for a couple of inches to extend above the top of the pan, folding the paper and cutting out the corners to fit the pan.)*

In a food processor, chop the walnuts with the sunflower seeds for 5 seconds.

In a large bowl, whisk the eggs together with the oil, honey, salt, and baking soda.

Mix in the almond flour and the chopped nuts to form a thick, heavy batter.

Spread the batter in the paper-lined pan, using a silicon spatula or damp fingers to flatten it into the corners of the pan.

Bake for 1 hour until nicely browned. (It will not rise as much as a normal loaf of bread.)

Remove the pan to a cooling rack and allow it to cool for 10 minutes. Lift the bread from the pan using the paper extensions. Peel off the paper and allow it to cool completely.

Wrap the loaf in plastic and store it in the refrigerator for up to a week or freeze it for up to a month.

*Omit seeds if you are in the early stages of the SCD and are still struggling with inflammation, as recommended in *Breaking the Vicious Cycle,* Page 79.

simple smoothie

Serves 2

Purée in a blender or food processor:
1 ripe banana, sliced
1 cup frozen, unsweetened fruit *(Cut large strawberries and peaches into smaller pieces.)*
1 cup SCD "legal" yogurt *(See instructions, page 68.)*
1-2 tsp. honey *(optional)*

strawberry jam

Makes about 1½ cups

10 oz. fresh or frozen unsweetened strawberries, thawed
½ cup honey

Chop the strawberries in a blender or food processor. Place the strawberries and the honey in a medium saucepan and simmer for 30-45 minutes, stirring frequently, until the jam is very thick.

Refrigerate the jam in a covered container. It will keep for up to a month.

Use as a topping for SCD pancakes, muffins, bread/toast, or SCD "legal" yogurt *(see instructions, page 68)*.

applesauce

fresh apples to fill a stockpot, ½ - ¾ full *(I recommend Gala, Braeburn, Empire, or Honey Crisp.)*
water
a pinch of salt
optional ingredients:
    fresh lemon juice
    ground cinnamon
    1 cup fresh, sliced strawberries
    honey
    unsalted butter

Wash and peel the apples—or leave the skins on if you like—then quarter and core them. Cut the apples into small chunks and place them in the stockpot. Sprinkle the apples with a little lemon juice to prevent them from turning brown—I don't bother, because I sprinkle them with cinnamon while they're cooking, which gives them a nice brown color.

Add enough water to coat the bottom of the stockpot (about a cup) and sprinkle the apples with the pinch of salt. Add cinnamon or strawberries if desired.

Cover the stockpot and bring the apples to a boil. Then turn down the heat to medium and simmer the apples, covered, stirring them every 10 or 15 minutes until they have "sauced," that is, until they are falling apart and will mash easily with a fork.

Mash the apples with a potato masher until they are the consistency that you like. Continue to simmer the sauce, uncovered, stirring it constantly until thick. Add honey to taste and if you want to be super-fancy, stir in a tablespoon of unsalted butter.

Let the applesauce cool a bit, and if you want it to be extra-smooth, purée it in small batches in a food processor or blender.

Serve the applesauce warm or cold. It can be refrigerated for up to a week or frozen for up to a month.

coleslaw - Amy McKenna
Serves 6-8

Combine in a large bowl:
  1 cup red cabbage, finely sliced
  3 cups green cabbage, finely sliced
  1 large carrot, grated
  2 green onions, minced

In a small bowl, whisk together:
  ¾ cup SCD "legal" mayonnaise* *(See recipe, page 18.)*
  ¼ cup SCD "legal" yogurt *(See instructions, page 68.)*
  2 T. neutral tasting vegetable oil *(I use grape seed oil.)*
  1 T. honey
  1 T. wine vinegar
  2 tsp. fresh lemon juice
  ½ tsp. dry mustard
  1 tsp. salt
  ⅛ tsp. black pepper

Toss the dressing with the cabbage mixture. Refrigerate the coleslaw until ready to serve.

*This mayonnaise contains raw egg yolks, therefore caution is advised due to the slight risk of salmonella or other food-borne illness. To reduce this risk, use fresh, properly refrigerated, Grade A eggs with intact shells; wash the outside of the shells before using, and avoid contact between the yolks and the shells.

cranberry sauce

Serves 8-10

½ cup honey
½ cup water or fresh orange juice
12 oz. fresh cranberries
grated lemon or orange rind *(optional)*

In a medium saucepan over medium heat, combine the honey with the water or orange juice. Stir in the cranberries and simmer until the cranberries pop *(about 10 minutes)*. Remove the sauce from the heat and allow it to cool. It will thicken as it cools.

Store the cranberry sauce covered, in the refrigerator. It will keep for up to a week.

Cranberry sauce may also be frozen for up to a month.

easy barbeque sauce
Makes about 5 cups

4 cups Tomato Purée *(See recipe below.)*
½ cup apple cider vinegar
½ cup honey
1 clove garlic, minced
½ tsp. red pepper flakes
2 tsp. smoked paprika
2 tsp. salt
½ tsp. black pepper

In a small saucepan, whisk together the Tomato Purée, vinegar, honey, and seasonings. Bring the sauce to a simmer and cook, whisking occasionally for 20 minutes, until thickened.

Tomato Purée: *(makes about 4 cups)* Quarter 12 Roma (plum) tomatoes and remove the seeds. Purée the tomatoes in a food processor. Pour the tomato purée in a saucepan and stir in one tablespoon olive oil. Bring the purée to a simmer and cook it for 1 hour, stirring frequently, until thickened. Let the purée cool for 5 minutes and return it to the food processor. Process for 3 minutes or until very smooth. Tomato Purée may be stored in an airtight container in the fridge for up to a week, or in the freezer for up to a month.

honey mustard salad dressing

Makes about ¾ cup

¼ cup red wine vinegar
½ cup olive oil
1 T. honey
1 tsp. dry mustard
1 tsp. dried basil
1 clove garlic, minced
1 tsp. salt
⅛ tsp. black pepper

Whisk all the ingredients together in a small bowl. Refrigerate the dressing for at least an hour to allow the flavors to blend. Whisk the dressing again just before serving.

The dressing may be stored in a covered jar in the refrigerator for up to a week. The olive oil will solidify in the refrigerator, so let the dressing stand at room temperature for several minutes to allow the olive oil to liquefy.

Shake well before serving.

mayonnaise*

Makes 1 cup
Have all ingredients at room temperature.

2 egg yolks
2 tsp. apple cider vinegar
2 tsp. honey
¼ tsp. dry mustard
½ tsp. salt
a dash of white pepper
1 cup neutral tasting vegetable oil *(I use grape seed or sunflower oil.)*

In a blender, combine the egg yolks with the vinegar, honey, dry mustard, salt, and pepper. With the blender running, slowly drizzle in the oil, a little at a time, until the mayonnaise is thick and creamy. Store in a covered container and refrigerate. Use the mayonnaise within 1 week.

*This mayonnaise contains raw egg yolks, therefore caution is advised due to the slight risk of salmonella or other food-borne illness. To reduce this risk, use fresh, properly refrigerated, Grade A eggs with intact shells; wash the outside of the shells before using, and avoid contact between the yolks and the shells.

mustard sauce

Makes about ⅔ cup

In a small bowl, whisk together to make a smooth sauce:
  ⅓ cup "legal" mayonnaise* *(See recipe, page 18.)*
  ⅓ cup SCD "legal" yogurt *(See instructions, page 68.)*
  1 tsp. dry mustard
  1½ tsp. apple cider vinegar
  ¼ tsp. salt
  1 green onion, minced

Serve with meat or fish.

Store in a covered container. Use mustard sauce within one week.

*This mayonnaise contains raw egg yolks, therefore caution is advised due to the slight risk of salmonella or other food-borne illness. To reduce this risk, use fresh, properly refrigerated, Grade A eggs with intact shells; wash the outside of the shells before using, and avoid contact between the yolks and the shells.

salsa

Makes 2-3 cups

3 large tomatoes, diced
1 small white onion, chopped
1 small red onion, chopped
6 green onions, chopped
¼ red bell pepper, chopped
1 jalapeno pepper, chopped
1 T. chopped fresh cilantro, to taste
½ cup apple cider vinegar
⅛ tsp. cayenne pepper
1 tsp. SCD "legal" chili powder*
¼ tsp. ground cumin
1 clove garlic, minced
1 T. fresh lemon juice
1 tsp. honey, to taste
1 tsp. salt, to taste
¼ tsp. black pepper

Combine all ingredients in a large bowl; refrigerate, and allow to sit for at least one hour. It's even better if made the day ahead.

Serve with "Nacho Chips," page 24.

---

*To make SCD "legal" chili powder: combine 5 T. ground, mild chili pepper *(available in ethnic groceries)*, 2 T. dried oregano, 1½ T. ground cumin, and ½ tsp. cayenne pepper. Store airtight.

tomato purée - a "legal" substitute for commercial tomato sauce
Makes about 4 cups

Quarter 12 Roma (plum) tomatoes and remove the seeds.

Purée the tomatoes in a food processor.

Pour the tomato purée into a saucepan; stir in one tablespoon olive oil.

Bring the purée to a simmer and cook it for 1 hour, stirring frequently, until thickened.

Let the purée cool for 5 minutes and return it to the food processor.

Process for 3 minutes or until very smooth.

Tomato Purée may be stored in an airtight container in the fridge for up to a week, or in the freezer for up to a month.

spinach salad with raspberry vinaigrette

For the Dressing: *makes about 1¼ cups*
 ½ cup fresh or frozen unsweetened raspberries, thawed
 4 T. honey
 ¼ cup red wine vinegar
 ⅛ tsp. ground cardamom or lemon zest
 ½ tsp. salt
 ¼ tsp. black pepper
 ½ cup neutral tasting vegetable oil *(I use grape seed oil.)*

For the Salad:
 Fresh spinach leaves
 Sliced fresh strawberries
 Pan toasted* raw sunflower seeds**

Blend the first 6 dressing ingredients in a food processor. With the machine running, slowly drizzle in the oil, processing the dressing until smooth and thick. Refrigerate leftover dressing in a covered jar for up to 2 weeks.

Drizzle the dressing over the salad ingredients and toss to combine.

*To toast sunflower seeds, heat them in a dry skillet over medium heat, stirring constantly until lightly browned. Transfer the seeds to a plate to cool completely.

**Seeds should not be consumed until symptom-free for 3 months. See *Breaking the Vicious Cycle*, page 79.

taco salad

Serves 4

olive oil
1 lb. ground beef or turkey
1 small onion, minced
1-2 T. SCD "legal" chili powder*, to taste
1 tsp. ground cumin
1 clove garlic, minced
¾ tsp. salt
¼ tsp. black pepper
pinch cayenne pepper
1 tomato, finely diced
½ cup water
assorted salad greens
additional salt and pepper
sliced black olives
sliced fresh tomatoes
SCD "legal" yogurt *(See instructions, page 68.)*
mild, block-type cheddar cheese, shredded *(Do not use packaged, pre-shredded cheese.)*
Guacamole *(See recipe below.)*

Generously coat a large skillet with olive oil. Heat the pan on medium to medium-high until the surface of the oil begins to shimmer. Brown the meat in the hot oil with the onion and seasonings, breaking up the meat with a spoon. Add the diced tomato and water and simmer until most of the juices are reduced.

Place the salad greens on dinner plates and drizzle with a little olive oil. Sprinkle with salt and pepper. Spoon the meat mixture on top of the greens and garnish with black olives, tomatoes, yogurt, cheese, and Guacamole. *(See recipe below.)* Nacho "Chips" go great with this. *(See recipe, page 24.)*

Easy Guacamole: Mash a ripe avocado with a ripe, chopped tomato, the juice of ½ lime, salt and pepper to taste, and a pinch or two of cayenne pepper if you like it hot.

***To make SCD "legal" chili powder:** combine 5 T. ground, mild chili pepper *(available in ethnic groceries)*, 2 T. dried oregano, 1½ T. ground cumin, and ½ tsp. cayenne pepper. Store airtight.

nacho "chips"
Makes 4-5 dozen

8 oz. mild cheddar cheese, cut into 1" squares, 1/8" thick
½ cup blanched almond flour
1 tsp. SCD "legal" chili powder*
⅛ tsp. black pepper
a dash of cayenne pepper

Line 2 cookie sheets with parchment paper. Arrange the cheese slices on the paper, 1" apart; allow them to come to room temperature.

Preheat the oven to 300° F.

In a small bowl, mix together the almond flour and the seasonings.

Sprinkle the cheese slices with the almond flour mixture and pat to coat evenly. Turn the cheese slices over and coat the other side.

Bake the cheese slices for 10-15 minutes until bubbly.

Leave the baked cheese slices on the cookie sheets until cool enough to handle. They will be quite soft—then transfer the cheese slices to paper towels to absorb oils; cool completely.

To "crisp" the chips, line 2 or more paper plates with parchment paper. Arrange 3 cheese slices on each plate and microwave, one plate at a time, on high, for 30-60 seconds. Watch them carefully so they do not burn. They will bubble up while cooking and develop a domed appearance.

Leave the chips on the parchment paper-lined plates until cool enough to handle, then stack them on clean paper towels to finish cooling. *(You may reuse the parchment-lined pape plates, since you will be microwaving several more batches.)*

Store the "chips" in an airtight container. Serve with "Salsa," page 20.

*To make SCD "legal" chili powder: combine 5 T. ground, mild chili pepper *(available in ethnic groceries)*, 2 T. dried oregano, 1½ T. ground cumin, and ½ tsp. cayenne pepper. Store airtight.

cheesy breadsticks
Makes 16-20

3 cups blanched almond flour
¾ cup grated, mild, block-type cheddar cheese *(Do not use packaged, pre-shredded cheese.)*
¼ cup (½ stick) unsalted, melted butter
½ tsp. baking soda
¾ tsp. salt
2 large eggs
¾ cup dry-curd cottage cheese*
¼ cup water
1 clove garlic, finely minced

Preheat the oven to 325° F.

Place the almond flour and cheese in a medium bowl. Blend all the other ingredients in a food processor until smooth. Spoon the blended ingredients into the bowl with the flour/cheese mixture and stir until well-combined.

Scoop out large tablespoons of dough; with wet hands form the dough into small breadstick shapes.

Place the breadsticks 1" apart on a cookie sheet that has been lined with parchment paper. Bake them for 15-20 minutes. They are done when golden brown, and a toothpick inserted into a breadstick comes out clean.

*Dry curd cottage cheese can be special-ordered from most full-service grocery stores.

spicy sausage snacks

Makes about 30

1 lb. ground pork
2 cloves garlic, minced
½ tsp. red pepper flakes or ¼ tsp. cayenne pepper
1 tsp. black pepper
¼ tsp. dried sage
½ tsp. dried basil
½ tsp. dried marjoram
½ tsp. dried oregano
1 tsp. salt
½ cup blanched almond flour
¾ cup grated, mild, block-type cheddar cheese *(Do not use pre-shredded, store-bought cheese.)*

Preheat the oven to 350° F.

Mix all ingredients with a fork until well-combined.

Moisten your hands with water and roll heaping tablespoons of the mixture between your palms to form balls, placing them on a baking sheet that has been lined with parchment paper.

Bake the sausage snacks for 20 minutes. *(Some of the cheese will ooze out onto the paper… that's okay.)* Drain the sausage snacks on paper towels. Serve hot or cold.

chicken soup

Serves 4

1½ lbs. chicken legs, thighs, or both
3-4 carrots, sliced
1 celery heart including leaves, sliced
2 cups fresh green beans, sliced in 1" pieces
1 small onion, sliced
1-2 cloves garlic, minced
1 bay leaf
½ tsp. dried sage
½ tsp. dried rosemary, crushed
½ tsp. dried thyme leaves, crushed
⅛ tsp. turmeric
2 tsp. salt
¼ tsp. black pepper
water
a double batch of Mini "Matzo Balls" if desired *(See recipe, page 28.)*

Place the chicken and vegetables in a 4-6 quart stockpot. Fill the pan with water to *just* cover the chicken and vegetables.

Add the seasonings and bring the soup to a boil over medium-high heat. Turn the heat down to low and cook, covered, 30 minutes or until the chicken is tender.

Remove the chicken to a dish and let it stand for 10 minutes or until cool enough to handle.

Remove the cooled chicken from the bones. Discard the skin and the bones. Slice or tear the meat into bite-sized pieces and set aside. Dispose of the bay leaf.

While the chicken is cooling, prepare the "matzo" balls. Bring the soup to a gentle boil and cook them, as directed on page 28, in the simmering soup.

Return the chicken to the soup; heat through and serve.

mini "matzo" balls

Serves 4

2 large eggs
1 tsp. grated onion
¼ tsp. salt
pinch black pepper
2-4 cups blanched almond flour

Beat together the eggs, onion, salt, and pepper.

Add the almond flour, stirring it in a quarter cup at a time until the mixture is the consistency of play-dough.

Pinch off small globs of dough with wet fingers and roll them between your palms into balls the size of small marbles. Set them on a plate.

Fill a medium saucepan ½ full with water and add 1 tsp. salt. Bring the water to a gentle boil. (Or you may cook the "matzo" balls in the chicken soup as described on page 27.)

Drop the "matzo" balls into the bubbling liquid. They will sink to the bottom, then float to the top.

Simmer them for 5 minutes, stirring occasionally.

Serve the "matzo balls" immediately or scoop them out with a slotted spoon to cool on layers of paper towels. Do not store them in leftover liquid or they will fall apart.

Re-heat leftover "matzo" balls, briefly, in simmering chicken soup, or gently boiling salted water.

creamy tomato soup
Serves 2

2 cups SCD "legal" *canned* tomato juice *(Heinz and Campbell's are free of illegal ingredients.)*
½ cup SCD "legal" yogurt *(See instructions, page 68.)*
1 tsp. butter
¼ tsp. salt, to taste
1 T. honey, to taste
a dash or two of black pepper

Whisk together all ingredients in a saucepan and heat slowly, stirring occasionally.

split pea soup

Serves 6-8
Soak the peas, as instructed, the night before.
Total cooking time: about 2 hours

1 lb. dried green split peas
2 T. olive oil
½ cup chopped onion
1 clove garlic, minced
½ tsp. dried oregano
1 bay leaf
2 tsp. salt
½ tsp. black pepper
4 cups sliced carrots
8 cups water
additional boiling water

Sort the peas, remove and dispose of debris. Place the peas in a large bowl and fill the bowl with cold water. Let the peas soak for 8-10 hours. Drain the peas and set aside, or refrigerate until ready to use.

In a 4-6 quart stockpot, heat the olive oil on medium to medium-high until the surface of the oil begins to shimmer. Sauté the onions, garlic, and seasonings in the hot oil until the onions are translucent, about 10 minutes.

Add the carrots, ½ of the split peas, and the water. Bring the pot to a boil; then turn down the heat to a simmer. Simmer the soup, uncovered, for 30-40 minutes, stirring occasionally.

Add the remaining split peas and continue to simmer the soup for another 30-40 minutes, or until the peas are soft. Add some boiling water if the soup gets too thick.

As it cooks, stir the soup frequently to prevent the solids from burning in the bottom of the pot. Remove the bay leaf. Taste the soup for salt and pepper and add more if needed.

good gravy
Makes about 2 cups—delicious on "Mashed Cauliflower 'Potatoes,'" page 32.

¼ cup (½ stick) unsalted butter
8 oz. fresh white mushrooms, sliced
½ cup SCD "legal" chicken stock *(no added starches, sugars, or gums)* or water
½ cup Almond Cream *(See recipe below.)*
turkey or chicken giblets *(optional)*
cooking water from giblets *(optional)*
additional water or stock as needed
¼ tsp. paprika
a pinch of nutmeg
salt and pepper, to taste

To prepare mushroom purée: *(This can be done a day ahead.)* In a large skillet, melt the butter on medium to medium-high until the foam begins to subside. Sauté the mushrooms in the butter until golden and crispy-brown around the edges. Turn off the heat and transfer the mushrooms to the work bowl of a food processor. Pour the stock or water into the skillet. *(Stand back! There will be a plume of steam when the cool liquid hits the hot skillet.)* On medium-high, cook and stir, loosening the browned bits in the bottom of the skillet. Take the pan off the heat and allow the resulting liquid to cool for 5 minutes; then spoon the liquid into the food processor. Purée the mushroom/stock mixture until very smooth, about 3 minutes, scraping the sides of the container as needed. Add the Almond Cream and process briefly to blend. Place the purée in a saucepan if planning to finish cooking the gravy right away. *(Or at this point the mixture can be refrigerated for later use.)*

To cook giblets: *(This is optional and can be done a day ahead.)* Place the giblets in a small saucepan of salted water. Bring the pan to a simmer. The liver will cook in about 5 minutes; cook it until it feels firm when poked with a sharp fork. The heart and gizzard will need to cook longer, until fork-tender—the gizzard up to 20 minutes. Add more liquid to the giblets as needed. Remove the cooked giblets to a dish to cool. Dice the cooked giblets; cover and refrigerate them. Reserve and refrigerate the cooking liquid for later use.

To prepare gravy: Place the mushroom purée in a saucepan. Add the diced giblets *(optional)*. Thin the gravy with the cooking water from the giblets, stock, or water. Add enough liquid to get the consistency you want. Bring the gravy to a simmer. Season with paprika, nutmeg, salt, and pepper to taste. The gravy may be frozen for later use.

Almond Cream: Place ¼ cup blanched almond flour and ¼ cup water in a food processor or blender. Purée for 3 minutes until very smooth.

mashed cauliflower "potatoes"
Serves 4-6

1 head cauliflower
¼-½ cup (½-1 stick) unsalted butter, softened
¼-½ cup SDC "legal" yogurt *(optional) (See instructions, page 68.)*
½ tsp. salt, to taste
¼ tsp. white pepper, to taste
½ cup grated, mild, block-type cheddar cheese *(optional) (Do not use packaged, pre-shredded cheese.)*

Preheat the oven to 350° F.

Cut up the cauliflower and cook it over boiling water in a steamer basket until fork tender—10-15 minutes.

Place the cooked cauliflower in a food processor and purée it until smooth with the butter and/or yogurt. Season with, salt, and white pepper, to taste. *(Yogurt will give the cauliflower a tangy flavor, or if you prefer, you can use butter alone. Try it topped with "Good Gravy," page 31.)*

Place the puréed cauliflower in a buttered baking dish, top it with cheddar cheese if desired, and bake it for 15-20 minutes, until the cheese melts.

oven baked stuffing

Serves 4-6

½ loaf "Lois Lang's Luscious Bread" (from *Breaking the Vicious Cycle* p.127)
½ cup (1 stick) unsalted butter
2-3 ribs celery, chopped
1 medium onion, chopped *(optional)*
8 oz. fresh mushrooms, roughly chopped
1 tsp. dried sage
½ tsp. dried thyme
a dash of nutmeg
a dash of cloves
1 cup chopped walnuts
½-1 cup hot water
salt and pepper, to taste
1 large egg, lightly beaten

Cut the bread into ½" cubes; spread them on cookie sheets that have been lined with parchment paper and toast them in a 170° F. oven for 90 minutes. Let the bread cubes cool completely in the oven. You may do this ahead and store the toasted bread cubes in an airtight container for several days.

In a large skillet, on medium to medium-high, heat the butter until the foam begins to subside. Sauté the celery, onions *(optional)*, and mushrooms in the butter until tender, 5-10 minutes. Remove the pan from the heat and stir in the sage, thyme, nutmeg, and cloves. Set aside.

Preheat the oven to 350° F.

Place the bread cubes and walnuts in a bowl and stir in the sautéed ingredients. Pour hot water over the stuffing, a little at a time, tossing it gently with a fork until the bread is moistened but not falling apart. Season the stuffing with salt and pepper to taste.

Gently fold in the beaten egg and bake the stuffing in a buttered baking dish for 30-40 minutes, until hot and browned on the top.

ratatouille
Serves 6-8

olive oil
1 medium onion, diced
1 large green pepper, diced
1-2 cloves garlic, minced
2 cups summer or zucchini squash*, cubed
2 cups eggplant*, cubed
2 large tomatoes, diced
salt and pepper
1 tsp. dried thyme
¾ cup Tomato Purée *(See recipe below.)*

In a large skillet that has a lid, heat a generous amount of olive oil on medium to medium-high until the surface of the oil begins to shimmer. Sauté the vegetables in the hot oil, in the order listed, salting and peppering lightly after each addition.

Cook and stir the mixture until the tomatoes begin to break down. Stir in the thyme. Cover the skillet, reduce the heat to a simmer, and cook the mixture for 30 minutes. Stir in the Tomato Purée and cook the mixture uncovered until heated through.

Taste for salt and add more if needed.

Serve the ratatouille chunky, or purée half of it in a food processor and return the puréed portion to the chunky portion. It's great all by itself with a sprinkle of grated, block-type Parmesan cheese *(do not use packaged, pre-grated cheese)* or as a side dish with meat or fish.

Tomato Purée: *(Makes about 4 cups.)* Quarter 12 Roma (plum) tomatoes and remove the seeds. Purée the tomatoes in a food processor. Pour the tomatoes into a saucepan and stir in one tablespoon olive oil. Bring the purée to a simmer and cook it for 1 hour, stirring frequently, until thickened. Let the purée cool 5 minutes and return it to the food processor. Process for 3 minutes or until very smooth. Tomato Purée may be stored in an airtight container in the fridge for up to a week, or in the freezer for up to a month.

*When shopping for eggplant and zucchini/summer squash, select small ones.
They will be less seedy and taste the best.

roasted butternut squash casserole
Serves 4-6

1 medium butternut squash
olive oil
honey
salt
black pepper
dried thyme
2-4 T. unsalted butter, melted
hot water

Preheat the oven to 375° F.

Peel the squash, slice it open, discard seeds and strings, and cut it into 1" chunks.

Scatter the squash on a foil-lined, rimmed baking sheet that has been coated with olive oil.

Drizzle the squash with olive oil and honey and toss to coat. Sprinkle the squash with salt, pepper, and thyme.

Roast the squash for 30-40 minutes, stirring it after 15 minutes, until fork-tender and nicely browned.

Remove the baking sheet to a cooling rack and cover it with foil, sealing the edges tightly. Let the squash cool to room temperature.

In a couple batches, transfer the squash to a food processor; purée it with the melted butter and enough hot water to moisten it to the desired consistency. Place each batch of puréed squash in a large bowl.

When all the squash is puréed, (it's okay if there are a few lumps) stir the squash to combine. Taste the squash purée; add more honey, melted butter, salt, or pepper if needed.

Transfer the squash purée to a greased casserole dish and bake, covered, in a preheated 350° F. oven for 30-40 minutes, until hot.

swiss chard*

Serves 4

1 lb. Swiss chard
olive oil
1 medium onion, sliced
1 clove garlic, minced
salt
black pepper
apple cider vinegar

Clean the chard leaves under running water; shake off the excess water. On a cutting board, fold the leaves in half, lengthwise, then trim out the center ribs with a sharp knife. Slice the ribs into 1" pieces and set them aside. Cut the leaves crosswise into approx. 3" pieces and set them aside, separate from the rib pieces.

Generously coat the bottom of a large skillet that has a lid with olive oil. Heat the oil on medium to medium-high until the surface of the oil begins to shimmer. Sauté the onion, garlic, and chard ribs in the hot oil until the stems begin to get tender, about 5-8 minutes, lightly salting and peppering them as they cook.

Add the leaves to the skillet, a couple handfuls at a time and stir until wilted, adding more leaves as each batch wilts. Splash the wilted leaves with a little apple cider vinegar. Reduce the heat to low and cover the skillet. Cook the chard until tender, 5-8 minutes. Salt to taste before serving.

*Variation: Clean and slice the chard leaves and ribs as instructed above. Omit the onion, garlic, and apple cider vinegar. Sauté the chard ribs and leaves in the olive oil with salt and pepper as instructed above. Splash the wilted leaves with a little dry white wine and sprinkle them lightly with ground nutmeg. Cover and cook as instructed above. Top the cooked chard with chopped pistachios and grated block-type Parmesan cheese. *(Do not use packaged, pre-grated cheese.)*

asian burgers

Serves 4-6

½ cup chopped, toasted pine nuts
1 egg
1 T. minced fresh garlic
2 green onions, minced
½ tsp. ground ginger
⅛ tsp. cayenne pepper
1 tsp. salt
¼ tsp. black pepper
1⅓ lbs. ground turkey or chicken
¼ cup blanched almond flour
grape seed oil

Toast the pine nuts in a dry skillet on medium-low until lightly browned. Transfer them to a dish to cool. Chop the toasted pine-nuts finely and set them aside.

In a small bowl, combine the egg and the seasonings. Place the meat, pine nuts, and almond flour in a medium bowl. Pour in the egg mixture and combine well with a fork. Refrigerate the meat mixture for at least one hour. Meanwhile, prepare the seasoned oil. *(See recipe below.)*

With wet fingers, form the meat mixture into 4-6 patties. Generously coat the bottom of a large skillet with the oil and heat it on medium to medium-high until the surface of the oil begins to shimmer. Sauté the patties in the hot oil until they are cooked through and nicely browned, about 5 minutes per side. *(The burgers also are great done on the grill—brush them with a little oil before grilling so they don't stick.)*

Serve burgers atop a bed of mixed greens. Dress with seasoned oil.

Seasoned oil:
⅓ cup grape seed oil
½ tsp. ground ginger
⅛ tsp. cayenne pepper
1 clove garlic, minced

Whisk all the ingredients together in a small bowl.

chicken paprika

olive oil
chicken thighs and/or drumsticks
salt
pepper
smoked paprika

Preheat the oven to 375° F.

Coat a shallow baking dish with olive oil. Use a dish large enough to allow at least 1" of space between the chicken pieces.

Rinse the chicken and pat it dry with paper towels, then place it in the baking dish and drizzle it with additional olive oil.

Brush the chicken with the oil until thoroughly coated, then sprinkle it generously on all sides with the seasonings.

Bake the chicken for 45 minutes, uncovered.

Transfer the chicken to a serving platter and cover it lightly with aluminum foil.

Let the chicken rest for 10 minutes before serving.

Serve topped with "Easy Barbeque Sauce," page 16.

crispy sautéed chicken breasts - Amy McKenna

Serves 4

1 lb. boneless, skinless chicken breasts, split
1 egg
olive oil
¼ cup blanched almond flour
salt and pepper
½ cup dry white wine
1 T. unsalted butter

Place each chicken breast between 2 piece of plastic wrap, and pound with a meat mallet to an even thickness, about ½".

Preheat the oven to 170° F. and place a heat-proof dish in the oven.

Mix the egg and 1 tsp. olive oil in a shallow dish. Spread the almond flour in another shallow dish.

Sprinkle each chicken breast with salt and pepper and then place it in the egg mixture, turning to coat both sides.

Lay the coated chicken breast in the almond flour mixture, turning to coat.

Generously coat the bottom of a large skillet with olive oil and heat it on medium to medium-high until the surface of the oil begins to shimmer.

Cook the chicken in batches so as not to crowd the pan; place the coated chicken breasts in the hot oil and cook the first side for 3-5 minutes, until nicely browned, then turn the chicken over and cook the second side for 3-5 minutes.

Remove each cooked chicken breast to the dish in the oven to keep warm.

With the stove turned off, add enough wine to fill the pan to a depth of about ¼". *There will be a plume of steam when the cool liquid hits the hot pan, so stand back.* Bring the wine to a boil; cook and stir until it thickens and reduces by about half. Lightly salt and pepper the sauce to taste. Turn off the heat and swirl in the butter.

Serve the cooked chicken topped with a spoonful of the wine sauce.

kick-me shrimp

Serves 4

olive oil
unsalted butter
1 lb. peeled, de-veined shrimp
2 cloves garlic, minced, divided
1 lb. asparagus, sliced in 1" pieces
2 fresh tomatoes, diced
dry white wine
salt
black pepper
cayenne pepper

Preheat the oven to 170° F. and place a 2-quart casserole in the oven. Pat the shrimp dry with paper towels.

Coat a large skillet with a generous amount of olive oil. Add a couple tablespoons of butter and heat the pan on medium to medium-high until the surface of the oil begins to shimmer and the butter foam begins to subside.

Add half of the minced garlic and the shrimp; sauté until the shrimp is pink and cooked through, about 3 minutes. Remove the shrimp with a slotted spoon to a dish and set aside.

Add the rest of the minced garlic to the skillet and sauté for 1 minute. Turn off the stove temporarily and add the asparagus, tomatoes, and ½ cup wine. Simmer, stirring occasionally, until the tomatoes break down, about 3-5 minutes. If the mixture seems dry, turn off the stove temporarily and add a little more wine. As the mixture cooks, season with salt, pepper, and a dash of cayenne pepper.

When the asparagus is tender, return the shrimp to the pan, and heat it through. With a slotted spoon, transfer the shrimp and vegetables to the casserole dish in the oven to stay warm while you make a simple wine reduction sauce with the pan juices.

With the stove turned off, add enough wine to fill the pan to a depth of about ¼". *(Stand back! There will be a plume of steam when the cool liquid hits the hot skillet.)* Bring the wine to a boil; cook and stir until it thickens and reduces by about half. Lightly salt and pepper the sauce to taste. Turn off the heat and swirl in a tablespoon of unsalted butter.

Serve the shrimp/vegetable mixture topped with a spoonful of the wine sauce.

lasagna
Serves 8

olive oil
5 medium zucchini
1 lb. ground beef
1 medium onion, chopped
2 cloves garlic, minced
4 cups Tomato Purée *(See recipe, page 21.)*
½ cup dry red wine
1 tsp. basil
1½ tsp. salt, divided
⅛ tsp. black pepper
16 oz. dry-curd cottage cheese*
¼ cup water
2 large eggs
2 cups grated block-type Parmesan cheese, divided *(Do not use pre-packaged, grated cheese.)*
1 T. chopped parsley
12 oz. sliced provolone cheese *(12 slices)*

Slice the zucchini in long, flat strips, a scant ¼" thick. Generously coat a large skillet with olive oil and heat on medium to medium-high until the surface of the oil begins to shimmer. Sauté the zucchini strips in the hot oil, in several batches, until golden brown. *(Do not crowd the pan, or the zucchini will not brown.)* Drain the zucchini strips on paper towels and set them aside.

In the same skillet, brown the ground beef with the onion and the garlic, breaking it up with a spoon. Add the Tomato Purée, wine, basil, 1 tsp. salt, and pepper. Simmer the meat sauce for 20 minutes.

In a medium bowl, combine the dry-curd cottage cheese, water, eggs, 1½ cups of the Parmesan cheese, the remaining ½ tsp. of salt, and the parsley.

Oil a 9 x 13" baking dish. Place a thin layer of the meat sauce in the bottom of the dish. Top with a layer of zucchini strips. Spread ½ of the cheese mixture over the zucchini. Layer 4 slices of provolone on top, cutting the provolone to fit the dish. Repeat layers of meat sauce, zucchini, cheese mixture, and provolone, ending with a layer of zucchini. Spread the zucchini with the remaining meat sauce and top with the remaining provolone. Sprinkle with the reserved Parmesan cheese.

Bake the lasagna at 375° F. for 45 minutes. Let it stand for 10 minutes before slicing.

*Dry curd cottage cheese can be special-ordered from most full-service grocery stores.

meatloaf
Serves 4-6

2 cups Tomato Purée *(See recipe below.)*
2 T. apple cider vinegar
6 T. honey
¼ tsp. cayenne pepper
½ tsp. black pepper
one small onion, grated
½ tsp. ground ginger
1¾ tsp. salt, divided
1 cup blanched almond flour
1 large egg
1 lb. ground chuck

Preheat the oven to 325° F.

In a small saucepan, whisk together the Tomato Purée, vinegar, honey, cayenne pepper, black pepper, onion, ginger, and 1 tsp. salt. Bring the sauce to a simmer and cook while whisking occasionally, for 5-8 minutes, until thickened. Let the sauce cool.

Combine the almond flour and ¾ tsp. salt in a large bowl. Stir in the egg and ¾ cup of the sauce. Add the ground chuck, combining with a fork until well-blended. Pack the mixture into a loaf pan that has been lined with parchment paper. *(Tear off a piece of paper big enough to allow for a couple of inches to extend above the top of the pan, folding and cutting out the corners to fit the pan.)*

Spread ¼ cup of the sauce on top of the meatloaf and bake for 1 hour. Allow the meatloaf to cool for at least 10 minutes, then use the paper extensions to lift the finished meatloaf out of the pan.

Warm the remaining sauce in a small saucepan. Top each slice of meatloaf with the warm sauce.

Tomato Purée: *(Makes about 4 cups.)* Quarter 12 Roma (plum) tomatoes and remove the seeds. Purée the tomatoes in a food processor. Pour the tomatoes into a saucepan and stir in one tablespoon olive oil. Bring the purée to a simmer and cook it for 1 hour, stirring frequently, until thickened. Let the purée cool for 5 minutes and return it to the food processor. Process for 3 minutes or until very smooth. Tomato Purée may be stored in an airtight container in the fridge for up to a week, or in the freezer for up to a month.

pizza

Makes one 10" pizza or two personal-sized pizzas

For the sauce:
1 cup Tomato Purée *(Recipe follows, page 44.)*
½ tsp. honey
½ tsp. dried basil
½ tsp. dried oregano
1 clove garlic, minced
½ tsp. salt, to taste
⅛ tsp. black pepper

In a small saucepan, whisk together the Tomato Purée, honey, and seasonings. Bring the sauce to a simmer and cook, whisking occasionally, for 5-8 minutes until thickened. Set the sauce aside.

For the crust:
1 large egg
1 tsp. olive oil
1 cup blanched almond flour
¼ tsp. salt
⅛ tsp. black pepper
¼ tsp. dried basil
¼ tsp. dried oregano

Preheat the oven to 325° F. Line a large baking sheet with parchment paper. In a medium bowl, combine all ingredients until a ball of dough comes together.

For one 10" pizza, flatten the ball into a large patty about ½" thick, dampening your fingers with water to prevent the dough from sticking to your hands. Place the dough patty in the center of the parchment-lined baking sheet. Place plastic wrap over the patty and roll it, on top of the wrap, with a rolling pin, into a circle about ⅛" thick.

For two personal-sized pizzas, divide dough into 2 balls, flatten them into patties about ½" thick, dampening your fingers with water to prevent the dough from sticking to your hands. Place the dough patties on the parchment-lined baking sheet, allowing room to roll out. Place plastic wrap over each patty and roll them, on top of the wrap, with a rolling pin, into two circles about ⅛" thick.

Carefully peel off the plastic wrap and bake the crust(s) for 15 minutes. Set the crust(s) aside.*

*Baked crusts may be stored in the fridge or freezer until ready to use.

To assemble the pizza: Raise the oven temperature to 400° F. Spread the sauce on the crust. Top the sauce with legal items of your choice: fresh mushrooms, olives*, green pepper, onion, homemade sausage *(see recipe, page 10)*, and thinly sliced provolone cheese.

Bake the pizza for 8-10 more minutes, until the cheese melts.

Tomato Purée: *(Makes about 4 cups.)* Quarter 12 Roma (plum) tomatoes and remove the seeds. Purée the tomatoes in a food processor. Pour the tomatoes into a saucepan and stir in one-tablespoon olive oil. Bring the purée to a simmer and cook it for 1 hour, stirring frequently, until thickened. Let the purée cool for 5 minutes and return it to the food processor. Process for 3 minutes or until very smooth. Tomato Purée may be stored in an airtight container in the fridge for up to a week, or in the freezer for up to a month.

*Olives must be free of added gums.

pork tenderloin
Serves 10-12

3 lb. pork tenderloin
olive oil
butcher's twine

Rub:

1 tsp. ground cloves
1 tsp. ground mace
1 tsp. ground nutmeg
½ tsp. ground allspice
½ tsp. ground cinnamon
2 tsp. paprika
1 tsp. dried thyme
½ tsp. dried sage
½ tsp. white pepper
1 tsp. salt

Have the pork at room temperature. Dry the pork with paper towels.

Tie the pork with butcher's twine, tucking the thin end under, creating a fairly even thickness.

Rub the pork with olive oil. In a small bowl, mix together the rub ingredients. Sprinkle the rub over the pork; then rub it into the surface of the pork.

Pat additional rub on the surface of the pork until the pork is well-coated. Store extra rub in an airtight container for future use.

Place a roasting pan in the oven and preheat it to 475° F.

Place the pork in the preheated pan and roast it for 25 minutes. Let the pork rest, covered with foil, for at least 10 minutes.

Slice the pork in ½" diagonal pieces and serve it with "Mustard Sauce," page 19.

pot roast

Serves 6-8
Total time: about 3½ hours

2-3 lb. boneless chuck roast, about 2" thick
olive oil
a bottle of dry red wine
water
4 cloves garlic, finely minced
1 T. salt
1 tsp. black pepper
8 large carrots peeled and cut in chunks
several tablespoons blanched almond flour

Preheat the oven to 325° F.

Dry the roast with paper towels. Generously coat the bottom of a large skillet with olive oil. Heat the oil on medium to medium-high until the surface of the oil begins to shimmer. Brown the roast on both sides in the hot oil. When it's nicely browned, place it in a covered roasting pan—a pan large enough to allow an inch or so of space surrounding the roast on all sides.

Turn off the stove. Pour off liquid fat from the skillet and dispose. Pour enough wine into the skillet to cover the bottom of the pan. *(Stand back! There will be a plume of steam when the cool wine hits the hot skillet.)* On medium-high, cook and stir the wine, loosening the browned bits in the bottom of the skillet. Pour the resulting liquid over the roast. Pour additional wine over the roast, to within ½" of the top of the roast. (If you run out of wine, you may use water.) Scatter the garlic, salt, and pepper over the roast.

Place the roasting pan in the preheated oven and bake, covered, for 3 hours, carefully turning the roast over after the first hour. Add boiling water if needed to raise the liquid level at least ½-way up the sides of the roast. Add the carrots for the last hour of cooking, adding more boiling water as needed to *just* cover the carrots.

When the roast is done it should be fork-tender and easy to pull apart. Carefully remove the roast and the carrots to a dish or tray. Cut the roast into serving-size chunks and remove/discard visible fat. Tilt the roasting pan and with a large spoon, skim large globules of liquid fat from the pan juices and discard. Place the roasting pan on a stovetop burner and bring the liquids to a simmer.

Add almond flour, 1 tablespoon at a time, cooking and stirring until the juices begin to thicken. Return the meat and carrots to the roasting pan and heat through.

pulled-pork barbeque
Serves 8-12

3 lbs. pork tenderloin
½ cup water
2 cloves garlic, minced
1 small onion, minced
1 tsp. smoked paprika
1 T. SCD "legal" chili powder*
2 tsp. salt
½ tsp. black pepper
Easy Barbeque Sauce *(See recipe below.)*

Place the pork in a crockpot. Pour in the water. Sprinkle the garlic, onion, paprika, chili powder, salt, and pepper on top. Cook the pork for 4-5 hours on low until the pork is very tender. Remove the pork to a large dish and pour the pot juices into another container. Return the pork to the crockpot and shred it with two forks.

Prepare the barbeque sauce. *(This can be done while the pork is cooking.)* Add ½ of the barbeque sauce to the pork and stir until combined. Add some of the pot juices if the mixture still seems dry. If necessary, re-heat the pork on high until heated through. Serve the pork topped with additional sauce.

Easy Barbeque Sauce
4 cups Tomato Purée *(See recipe page 21.)*
½ cup apple cider vinegar
½ cup honey
1 clove garlic, minced
½ tsp. red pepper flakes
2 tsp. smoked paprika
2 tsp. salt
½ tsp. black pepper

In a medium saucepan, whisk together the Tomato Purée, vinegar, honey, and seasonings. Bring the sauce to a simmer and cook for 20 minutes, whisking occasionally, until thickened.

---

*To make SCD "legal" chili powder: combine 5 T. ground mild chili pepper *(available in ethnic groceries)*, 2 T. dried oregano, 1½ T. ground cumin, and ½ tsp. cayenne pepper. Store airtight.

chewy monster cookies

Makes about 4 dozen

½ cup (1 stick) unsalted butter, softened
¾ cup honey
1 large egg, lightly-beaten
½ tsp. baking soda
¼ tsp. salt
1 tsp. ground cinnamon
1 tsp. "legal" vanilla extract *(no added sugars)*
3 cups blanched almond flour
1 cup raisins
1 cup chopped walnuts or pecans
1 cup unsweetened, shredded coconut

Preheat the oven to 325° F.

Mix the ingredients in the order listed and drop the dough by heaping tablespoons onto cookie sheets that have been lined with parchment paper. Flatten each dough glob with dampened fingers.

Bake the cookies for 15-20 minutes until golden-brown. Cool them for 10 minutes on the cookie sheets, then transfer them to wire racks. When completely cool, store the cookies in an airtight container.

They freeze well.

cut-out cookies

Makes 3-4 dozen, depending on the size of cookie cutters

½ cup (1 stick) unsalted butter, softened
½ cup honey
1 large egg, lightly-beaten
¼ tsp. salt
1 tsp. baking soda
spices as desired *(see below)*
3½ cups blanched almond flour
additional almond flour as needed for rolling pin and cutting surface

For ginger cookies use:
1½ tsp. ground ginger
½ tsp. ground cloves
1 tsp. ground cinnamon

For "sugar" cookies use:
1½ tsp. ground nutmeg

Cream together the butter and honey. Add the lightly-beaten egg, salt, baking soda, and spices as desired. Add the almond flour and stir until well-combined. Divide the dough in thirds and scrape/dump it onto three large sheets of plastic wrap. Fold the sides of the wrap loosely over the dough and press it down into flat patties roughly ½" thick. Refrigerate the dough 1 hour or more.

Preheat the oven to 325° F.

Sprinkle both sides of one of the dough patties with almond flour. Sprinkle almond flour on the counter top or a wooden pastry board. Roll out the dough ¼" thick, lifting the dough while rolling and sprinkling a little more almond flour underneath to prevent the dough from sticking to the work surface. *(A little sticking is unavoidable.)*

Cut the dough with cookie cutters that have been dipped in almond flour. With a spatula *(silicone works the best),* transfer the cut-outs carefully to a cookie sheet that has been lined with parchment paper. Place the cookies 1" apart. Gather the dough scraps into a ball and re-roll. If the dough becomes too soft, return it to the refrigerator until firm. Repeat the rolling and cutting with the remaining dough patties. Combine the dough scraps and continue to roll and cut until finished.

Bake the cookies, one sheet at a time, for 7-10 minutes, until they are lightly browned at the tips and edges. When firm enough to handle, remove the cookies to wire racks with a spatula. Turn the oven off and let the cookies cool completely. Save the parchment paper.

To crisp the cookies: Preheat the oven to 170° F. Arrange the cookies on parchment paper-lined cookie sheets—you can reuse the same paper you used before. Bake for 1 hour and then turn off the oven. Let the cookies cool in the oven. When the oven is cool, the cookies will be crisp. Store the cookies in an airtight container for up to two weeks. (If the cookies soften you can "re-crisp" them by putting them in a 170° F. oven for 15 minutes, letting them cool in the oven.)

peanut butter brownies* - Amy McKenna

1¼ cups *(100% peanut)* crunchy peanut butter
½ cup honey
1 large egg
1 tsp. "legal" vanilla extract *(no added sugars)*
½ tsp. baking soda
¼ tsp. salt

Preheat the oven to 300° F.

In a medium bowl, combine all ingredients. Butter the bottom of an 8 x 8" baking pan, then line it with parchment paper. *(Tear off a piece of paper big enough to allow for a couple of inches to extend above the top of the pan, folding the paper and cutting out the corners to fit the pan.)*

Spread the batter in the paper-lined pan.

Bake the brownies for 30 minutes, or until the edges are nicely browned. Cool the brownies in the pan for 20 minutes, then use the parchment paper extensions to carefully remove them to a wire rack. When the brownies are completely cool, carefully peel off the paper, and cut them into 1" squares.

Store the brownies in an airtight container for up to a week or wrap them in plastic and freeze them for up to a month.

*When first trying these, it is a good idea to limit your intake to two per day.
They are so delicious, people have been known to eat a whole batch in two or three days,
which can cause a flare-up, especially early on in the diet.

pecan crispies

Makes about 4 dozen

½ cup (1 stick) unsalted butter, melted
1 large egg, lightly-beaten
1½ lb. pecans, roughly chopped
¾ cup honey
1 tsp. "legal" vanilla extract *(no added sugars)*
½ tsp. salt
½ cup blanched almond flour

Preheat the oven to 300° F.

Lightly butter the bottom of an 11 x 17" jelly roll pan. Line the pan with parchment paper. *(Tear off a piece of paper big enough to allow for a couple of inches to extend above the top of the pan, folding and cutting out the corners to fit the pan.)*

In a large bowl, combine the ingredients and spread the mixture evenly in the paper-lined pan.

Bake for 20-25 minutes until bubbly all over and starting to firm up. Remove the pan from the oven and place it on a cooling rack. Loosen the edges of the slab from the paper with a table knife.

When completely cool, using the paper extensions, gently lift the slab in one piece to a cutting board. With a sharp knife, cut it in squares and transfer them carefully to cookie sheets lined with parchment paper, spacing them ½" apart. The crispies are quite delicate at this point and may tend to break apart. If so, gently press them back together with your fingers.

Bake the crispies at 170° F. for 3 hours. Let them cool in the oven. They will continue to crisp as they cool. If they are still not crisp when cool, reheat the oven to 170° F. and bake for another 30 minutes. Stored airtight, they will stay crisp for a couple weeks. (If the cookies soften you can "re-crisp" them by putting them in a 170° F. oven for 15 minutes, letting them cool in the oven.)

pumpkin pie

Makes one 9" pie
This pie uses "Fresh Pumpkin Purée," which should be made the day ahead—recipe on page 53.

Crust:

1½ cups *cold* blanched almond flour
⅛ tsp. salt
¼ cup (½ stick) *cold*, unsalted butter
1-2 T. ice water
1 large egg yolk, for egg wash

Place the almond flour and salt in the work bowl of a food processor. Blend briefly. Cut the cold butter into 8 pieces and scatter them over the almond flour. Pulse several times until the mixture resembles coarse meal interspersed with many pea-sized lumps. While running the processor, trickle in the ice water through the feed tube *just* until the dough begins to gather together and form a mass. Stop processing.

Dump/scrape the dough out onto a large piece of plastic wrap; then, by lifting the sides of the wrap, form the dough into a rough ball shape. Fold the sides of the wrap loosely over the ball and press it down into a flat patty, roughly 8" in diameter. *(You may notice small lumps of butter throughout the dough—that's okay.)* Refrigerate the dough patty for 30 minutes.

Generously butter a 9" glass pie plate. Place the dough patty in the center of the plate, plastic wrap side up, and begin to gently work the dough *(through the wrap)* across the bottom, up the sides, and onto the rim. If cracks develop, press them together through the plastic wrap. Continue working the dough until it's a fairly even thickness. *(This might take a few minutes. It helps to hold the pie plate up to a bright light to see if there are any spots that are too thin or too thick.)* Refrigerate the crust for at least 30 minutes with the plastic wrap in place.

Preheat the oven to 325° F.

Carefully peel off the plastic wrap and prick the crust all over with a fork. Then bake it for 10-15 minutes until the edges *just* begin to brown a little and the crust firms up. Check it for air bubbles from time to time while it bakes, poking large ones with a fork. Remove the crust from the oven.

Add a little water to the egg yolk and mix until it's a "paintable" consistency. Brush the bottom and sides of the crust gently with the egg yolk "paint." *(I use a soft silicone basting brush.)* Be careful to not tear the *very* delicate surface of the crust. Return the crust to the oven for 2 minutes or until the egg wash has set. Allow the crust to cool completely before filling.

Filling: *(This filling is also delicious "crustless." Just pour the mixture into a well-buttered 9" pie plate and bake as directed.)*

    2 large eggs, lightly-beaten
    ½ cup honey
    1 tsp. "legal" vanilla extract *(no added sugars)*
    1½ cups Fresh Pumpkin Purée *(See recipe below.)*
    1½ tsp. ground cinnamon
    ½ tsp. ground nutmeg
    ½ tsp. ground ginger
    ⅛ tsp. ground cloves
    ¼ tsp. salt
    1 cup Almond Cream *(See recipe below.)*

Preheat the oven to 325° F.

In a large bowl, whisk the eggs with the honey and vanilla until well-blended. In a medium bowl, combine the Fresh Pumpkin Purée, spices, and salt. Add the pumpkin mixture to the egg mixture, stirring until well-blended. Stir in the Almond Cream; mix well. Pour the mixture into the prepared crust. Cover the edges of the crust with strips of aluminum foil. Bake for 1 hour. Let the pie cool completely on a wire rack. Refrigerate the pie before cutting. Top it with "Whipped French Cream." *(See page 68 for instructions.)*

Almond Cream: *makes about 1 cup*
    ¾ cup water
    ¾ cup blanched almond flour

Place the almond flour and water in a food processor or blender. Purée for 3 minutes until very smooth.

Fresh Pumpkin Purée: Preheat the oven to 400° F. Halve 2 small "pie pumpkins" *(available in autumn in larger grocery stores).* Remove the seeds and strings. Place the pumpkins cut-side-down on a large, rimmed baking pan. Pour enough water in the pan to *just* cover the bottom of the pan. Cover the pan with another sheet of foil and seal the edges of the foil completely. Poke a couple holes in the foil to vent it. Bake the pumpkins for 45-60 minutes until fork-tender. *(I poke a sharp fork right through the foil to test for doneness.)* Remove the pan to a cooling rack. Carefully open one corner of the foil to let the steam escape. Let the pumpkins stand until cool enough to handle. Scrape the flesh away from the skin and place the flesh in a food processor. Purée it until smooth. Transfer the purée to a colander or sieve that has been lined with a coffee filter or cheesecloth and set it atop a large bowl. Refrigerate the bowl and let the purée drip for several hours or overnight. Discard liquid. Freeze leftover purée for later use.

scd baking tips... is it done yet???

Baking **Specific Carbohydrate Diet** items can be quite a learning curve. I've had my successes and my flops, but bird-dog that I am, I'm not one to give up until I figure things out—so here's a compilation of things I've learned in the process. And I must give credit where credit's due—my daughter **Amy**, has been my long-distance baking buddy, collaborating with me on many of the recipes in *Turtle Soup*.

One of the initial challenges: knowing when baked goods are done. At first, I was producing muffins and cookies that were burned on the outside and goopy in the middle. Then I learned that the recipes in the **SCD** "bible," *Breaking the Vicious Cycle*—my first experience baking with **blanched almond flour***—were written before the advent of digital ovens. (Apparently, older ovens, when set at 350° F. were really closer to 325° F.) I have found that most of the **sweet** baked goods in **BTVC** bake much more evenly at 300-325° F., requiring maybe 10-15 minutes longer in the oven. (350° F. is still fine for savory baked goods.)

And what to do when trying to manipulate the stickier **SCD** dough? Slightly wet fingers work splendidly for shaping and smoothing the top of **breads** and flattening **cookies** and **rolls**—or if you don't like to get messy, use a silicone spatula.

Here's a neat way to simplify the bread baking routine. Use **parchment paper** to line bread pans—the loaf pops right out—no need to butter the pan and saves time on the clean up too! Tear off a piece big enough to allow for a few inches of paper to extend above the top of the pan, folding and cutting out the corners to fit the pan—then use the paper extensions to lift the finished loaf out of the pan. This works very well with **"Lois Lang's Luscious Bread,"** one of our favorites in the recipe section of *Breaking the Vicious Cycle*.

It also helps to lightly oil the cup when measuring honey—the honey slides right out. And a **Pampered Chef Measure-All Cup** is really great for measuring sticky-stuff like honey and peanut butter—this nifty gadget has an inner plunger that pushes out the contents from underneath—then a simple scrape with a spatula gets all the sticky yumminess into the mixing bowl. I also swear by **Pampered Chef Scoops** for evenly depositing doughs and batters in their respective baking pans.

Sometimes a batter or dough seems overly wet. Egg sizes may vary and altitude can cause variations in moisture content, so it's okay to add a little more almond flour—but too much almond flour will cause an overly dense product. Also, always gently **pack** almond flour when measuring to be sure there are no air pockets.

---

*Blanched almond flour should be stored in the refrigerator. It can be stored, refrigerated, for up to 3 months, or it can be stored in the freezer for up to a year.

Eggs are the glue that hold **SCD** baked goods together—eggs also function as leavening, so I recommend lightly beating eggs (I try to have them at room temperature) before adding them to a recipe—a tenderer, lighter product will result.

Baking soda is the only other leavening allowed on the **SCD** and it reacts with acid ingredients (like yogurt and vinegar) so adding a couple teaspoons of homemade **SCD "legal"* yogurt**** to a recipe might make it rise better. Also, be sure your baking soda is fresh and stored in an airtight container.

Since honey is a natural antibacterial/antifungal agent, sweet **SCD** baked goods can keep at room temperature in sealed containers for up to a week, or refrigerated for up to 2 weeks. Savory baked goods should be kept under refrigeration to retard spoilage. All **SCD** baked goods freeze well, if tightly wrapped, for several months.

And now for that all-important question: **"Is it done yet?"** In my experience, baking temperature is the most important factor, and as I mentioned before **300-325° F.** seems to be best for sweet baked goods. You may have to experiment to find the optimal setting for your oven. The signs of baked goods being done are: springy and firm to the touch, nicely browned, a toothpick inserted in the center comes out clean, starting to pull away from the sides of the pan, and even falling a bit. (It's perfectly normal for **SCD** baked goods to fall a little.) Also, I've noticed that all sweet baked goods taste even better the next day!

*For a list of legal and illegal foods for the Specific Carbohydrate Diet™, see: *Breaking the Vicious Cycle: Intestinal Health through Diet, p.p.73-8,* or visit: http://www.breakingtheviciouscycle.info/legal/legal_illegal_a-c.htm

**See "Appendix 3," page 68, for information about making yogurt.

appendix 1 - blog posts

Our Specific Carbohydrate Diet™ journey began in February of 2007. Amy and I blogged about our experiences with the diet—as Amy's "Diet Buddy" for her first year on the diet, I lent moral support and encouragement, helping her figure out this new way of cooking and eating, while she SCD'd her way through two happy and healthy pregnancies—not without their unique challenges—finding an SCD-sympathetic obstetrician/hospital; testing for gestational diabetes (routine), requiring the consumption of a sugary syrup, not recommended on the SCD; and the necessity of establishing optimal nutrition for both pregnancy and lactation. The following blog posts were written during our mutual journeys…

Beth Spencer - bethsblog - http://bethsblog.typepad.com

Diet Buddies   02/07/07

My daughter has suffered from Crohn's disease since high school.
Tummy pain. Fatigue. General malaise.
There has been an increase in her symptoms
in the past few months.

She's seen the top gastroenterologist in the Midwest.
He's thrown medicine at it that has helped to a degree.
She wants to have another baby but doesn't
want to be on medication.
He wants her to stay on the meds.
But the long term side effects are a little scary.
Short term it causes immune system suppression. Fatigue. Sun sensitivity.
Long term, there's a risk of cancer.
The jury's out regarding the possible effects on a fetus.

The other day, she talked to a friend of mine who also has Crohn's.
My friend suggested the SCD.
Yes: eggs, cheese, meats, nuts, fruits, veggies, yogurt.
No: grains, starches, refined sugar.
None at all.
A little honey is okay.
A giant paradigm shift for my daughter.
(I decided to be her Diet Buddy and do it with her for moral support.)
She jumped in with both feet.
3 days later my grown-up little girl is feeling better.
My fingers and toes are crossed.

A Month without Bread   03/07/07

Daughter Amy and I continue to eat according to the Specific Carbohydrate Diet™, as outlined in the book, *Breaking the Vicious Cycle: Intestinal Health through Diet.* (BTVC) We are learning how to bake muffins, cookies, and "bread" with almond flour instead of wheat. The other night, Amy made lasagna with zucchini strips in place of noodles and it was pronounced delicious by her husband, Stephen.

One unique challenge of SCD baking is producing a product that is neither burned nor raw, and there's a fine line between these two extremes. SCD muffins are an important part of the diet—main ingredients being almond flour and honey, both of which have a tendency to burn, so oven temperatures need to be kept low. Bread ingredients include dry-curd cottage cheese and eggs, so the baked goods are at their best moist and tender, at their worse charred on the outside and gooey on the inside. If baked successfully, the SCD breads are firm yet tender and can be sliced, toasted, buttered, and jammed (*Turtle Soup,* "Strawberry Jam," page 12) or made into nice little sandwiches.

This has been an interesting learning curve for us both. We've been experimenting with and reworking the recipes in BTVC, creating variations of our own, and exchanging emails and phone calls many times a day—maybe we'll publish a cookbook someday!

The other challenge is time. Things like ketchup, jam, sauces and dressings, all baked goods, and yogurt (which requires a 24 hr. culture to eliminate lactose) must be made from scratch. Almost all commercial products contain banned substances like sugars, starches, and gums. ALL labels must be read carefully and both of us have done major cupboard and refrigerator purges. It has been fun commiserating with Amy while doing all these experiments. Soon we will become experts and a natural rhythm will develop.

You might ask how our husbands are tolerating this insanity. They have graciously supported us and mostly applauded our efforts. Stephen is so happy that Amy is feeling better. And he has never eaten more fruits and veggies in his life. My husband, Gary, has never been one to complain or comment much about his grub. When asked he says, "I like it." (Hey Mikey!)

The super great news is that Amy is feeling MUCH BETTER. She has been able to reduce and then quit her medication over the past month. She is free of Crohn's symptoms most of the time. She has been following the diet RELIGIOUSLY. Her energy level and appetite has increased dramatically, which is a good thing because her darling toddler is running her ragged, and guess what—she wants to have another baby!

Two Month's Without Bread   04/10/07

It's been two months since I embarked on the SCD, in solidarity with my daughter who has Crohn's disease. Even though I thought I was doing the SCD to support Amy, I found myself benefiting from following the diet too. The first month I experienced significant improvement of chronic knee arthritis and skin inflammation, and a reduction of intestinal gas and bloating.

Together my daughter and I are getting consistent and delicious results with the almond flour baked goods. I've been experimenting with using egg white in place of all or part of the egg called for in the recipes with good success. Since my husband is also eating SCD baked goods and has to watch his cholesterol, this seemed to be a good option. What works best for me with egg white is to measure, allowing 3 tablespoons egg white for each egg called for in SCD baked goods.

I hit one small bump. Two weeks ago my stomach started hurting—up under my ribs on the left side—especially after eating nuts or nut flour baked goods. Last week I went to see my doctor. She said that with the dramatic changes to my diet over the past 2 months I may well have annoyed either my stomach or my gall bladder. She ran some blood tests. The Doc said to take Pepcid, eat only what doesn't aggravate my stomach, and stay away from nuts for a while, which pretty much eliminates my beloved SCD baked goods and leaves me with eggs, lean meats, yogurt, cheese, fruits, and veggies.

In the midst of this confusion, I made a one-day foray into the world of grain. I had a piece of homemade whole wheat toast, which tasted weird—and this was a bread that I had loved and eaten almost daily before starting the SCD. That same day I had a little brown rice and a couple oatmeal cookies made with honey and whole wheat—they tasted strange to me too after eating SCD muffins and cookies for 2 months. Within a few hours of eating the grain products, my belly was all filled up with gas.

The test results for gall bladder and stomach ulcer came back normal. After about a week of not eating any nuts or nut flour baked goods, I was able to tolerate a small piece of SCD Caramel Pecan Coffee Cake (*Turtle Soup,* page 6) at Easter brunch. I also discovered that I digest the nut flour products better if I chew them thoroughly, eat slowly, and have a little water with them. In fact, I probably haven't been drinking enough water in general.

Last week I emailed Raman Prasad at www.scdrecipes.com and he concurred that I probably overdid the nut flour baked goods. Raman recommended that I reduce them to one-a-day and maybe work up to two-a-day, eventually. He also suggested that I keep a food journal. So after much consternation, I have determined stay with the SCD. My joints, skin, energy level, and overall mood is very good. My irritated stomach is healing. I need to pay closer attention and listen to my body in order to find the right food balance for me.

It's a process... a lot like many things in life.

Six Months Without Bread   08/14/07

On February 3, according to my journal, I began the Specific Carbohydrate Diet™ (SCD). So, technically it's been 7 months, if you subtract the month that I experimented with gluten-free eating. But for the past 2 months, I've been sticking with the SCD, being more cautious with the almond flour products, which seemed to have been irritating my stomach and I feel better than ever. My gut is quiet unless "nature is calling." My inflammatory issues: rosacea and osteoarthritis are all <u>vastly</u> improved.

Yesterday, I heard from a mother whose 13-year-old son is struggling with ulcerative colitis. He's feeling better on the SCD, but is having a hard time with the food restrictions. Oh, how he longs for a slice of pizza—with a normal crust—not an ersatz almond flour one. I remember how strange the almond baked goods tasted at first, and how much easier it would have been to make a sandwich with a slice of regular bread.

Last week, I spoke with Lucy at Lucy's Kitchen Shop. She has followed the SCD for 15 years and feels wonderful—it is her "normal". It really helped to talk with someone who has been following the SCD successfully for so long.

It also really helps to have a Diet Buddy. My daughter, Amy, who has Crohn's, has been on the SCD since February too—so she and I have our own little support group. (By the way, she's now off all meds, in her 20th week of pregnancy, and feeling great.) I'm fortunate that my husband is doing the SCD along with me, so I don't have to cook two different ways. I have to give my daughter extra-credit, though, for she has "normal" eating family members under her roof—one who is a triathlete, (and we all know how they need their pasta!) so she must resist temptation much more often than I. But she says that when tempted, she knows that forbidden foods will make her feel sick, and for her, it's just not worth it.

So, if you are a fellow SCDer, take heart. What you are doing is not easy—simple—but not easy. Expect an adjustment period, and also a sense of grieving the loss of some of your favorite foods. On the upside, you really do get used to this new way of eating. The rewards of feeling so good are so worth it! Lucy assured me that in time it <u>will</u> all seem normal.

Amy McKenna - RoboRanch - http://www.roboranch.com

Not Thinking about My Gut   03/15/07

Back in high school, when the specialist took a tissue sample of a never-closing anal fistula that was, quite literally, a pain in the butt, he determined that I had a condition called Crohn's Disease, a type of inflammatory bowel disease that can affect any part of the gastrointestinal tract. He said that I should be prepared for a future with diarrhea and gut pain. Chronic. Embarrassing. Incurable. At seventeen, I wasn't ready to hear this. So I ignored it as best I could.

Shortly after graduating from college, I began to notice my gut a little more than usual. It started with the feeling that I had to use the bathroom all the time. This was highly inconvenient, since I was employed as a secretary and couldn't leave my station unless I bugged my busy manager to cover the phones. So I'd wait as long as I could, sitting uncomfortably at my desk, trying to hide the pain. Sometimes I felt a stabbing, heartburn sensation. Other times I felt filled up with gas all the way to my eyeballs. No matter how many times I used the bathroom, I seldom felt relief.

At some point, my high school Crohn's diagnosis crossed my mind, but I tried to avoid it. I decided the problem had to be something simple, like lactose intolerance. After a month of dairy avoidance and an inconclusive food diary, feeling clueless and helpless, I made an appointment with a gastroenterologist at the University of Michigan. He scheduled a colonoscopy and a few other unpleasant procedures. Quickly and emphatically, his judgment was: Crohn's. He said that my intestine was very narrowed with inflammation and that if it had gotten much worse, I may have needed surgery. He put me on two medications: Prednisone, which is a steroid designed to reduce inflammation, and a maintenance drug called Pentasa.

The Prednisone worked well. I had never felt better. But its side effects made it an unwise long-term medication. Once I stopped taking it, I felt bad again. I stuck with the Pentasa for a while, but it really didn't help much. So, in came the stronger artillery—6MP, an immunosuppressant drug to help the body stop fighting itself. It eased the pain, but the tradeoffs were a weakened immune system, fatigue, sun sensitivity, and unknown long-term side effects—possibly cancer. I stayed on it for a couple of years because it was better than hurting all the time. But in 2004, Stephen and I wanted to get pregnant.

6MP, a class D drug, has not been tested enough to know if it's safe for pregnancy or breastfeeding. So, I decided to go off the medication before getting pregnant. It turned out to be a good pregnancy, but I started feeling sick six months after baby Sophia was born. I desperately wanted to continue breastfeeding, so I told myself I could make it until Sophia was one year old. Right before her first birthday, I scheduled an emergency appointment with my gastro doctor. He put me back on another round of Prednisone and 6MP, which helped clear things up. I felt great for six months, and then we started thinking about baby #2.

Since I was feeling better, I wanted to go off the 6MP for the second pregnancy. But my gastro doctor advised against it, feeling that the risk of a flare while pregnant was worse than the potential risks of staying on the medicine. He said many women were staying on it and seeing no ill effects on the fetus. I think he could sense my hesitancy because he suggested I try a half dose for a while to see how it felt. When I tried cutting back, I felt sick almost immediately. And in the meantime, I'd gotten a second opinion from a high-risk maternal-fetal medicine OB. He wanted me off the meds. My family doctor also thought they were pretty risky for pregnancy. I wanted to believe them—to pretend I'd be okay if I stopped the medication. But back on the full dose of 6MP, my gut was still giving me trouble. I felt stuck; no options. I was beginning to let go of the denial. Acceptance was sobering.

So, here I was, feeling confused and stressed and hopeless, and now my gut was acting up even while I was on the 6MP. My wise mother suggested I talk to her friend who has been living with Crohn's for many years and has five kids. This lovely, helpful woman told me about a diet she'd been following called The Specific Carbohydrate Diet™ (SCD) based on the book, *Breaking The Vicious Cycle: Intestinal Healing Through Diet,* by Elaine Gottschall. After hearing my mom's friend's story about her horrible dealings with Crohn's disease and intestinal surgery, and how she turned her life around with the SCD, I knew I had to give it a try.

A few web searches later, I'd found hundreds of glowing reviews written by people with health issues like mine. And there were many Internet support groups and forums for the SCD and even a website based on the book. I immediately bought the book and a yogurt* maker (a key for the diet), and I started eating very differently than ever before. In the past, I'd always had at least one grain with every meal, and this diet didn't allow for ANY grains. Instead, I could eat: vegetables (except for potatoes and sweet potatoes); meat; fruit; fermented, low-lactose/low-sugar dairy; nuts and seeds; some dried beans; honey; butter; and plant oils. No soy, grains, sugar, starches, or many other additives that are found in pre-packaged, processed foods.

The idea behind the SCD is that the gut is easily able to digest monosaccharides, so people with intestinal issues should stick with simple carbs. Stop bombarding the gut with extra sugars and starches, and healing will be able to take place. I've been strictly following this plan since February 5, 2007, and I'm feeling really, amazingly great! It was hard at first—I felt like I was mourning the death of a loved one (bread! cookies! pasta! chocolate!!!!)—and I had a hard time re-thinking all of my tried-and-true recipes. Plus, I believe my body was in detox mode for the first week, since I felt really tired and spacey, but I did notice less bloating and gas right away. And now I'm not running to the bathroom more than once a day, which is lovely! The other great thing—no, the BEST thing—is that I'm totally off my medication and feeling good for the first time in a long time. There are more and more days where I don't think about my gut at all, where I feel like a person instead of a disease. This is new for me, and it's wonderful.

I have faith that I will be able to enjoy a medication-free, healthy pregnancy if I stay on the SCD. It's very empowering to find that I can control and possibly cure my illness simply by being careful about what I put into my body. For that, I can give up pasta; I can even give up chocolate!

P.S. Thanks, Mom, for being my SCD buddy.

*Instructions for SCD "legal" yogurt can be found on page 68 of *Turtle Soup.*

Three Down, Six to Go   06/18/07

As of last Tuesday, I'm officially out of the first trimester of my second pregnancy. Woo hoo! This week I have much more energy, much less need to urinate every 5 seconds, and much relief that I'm supposedly in the safe-zone now.

I can't even begin to express how happy I am that I'm on the Specific Carbohydrate Diet™ (SCD) and that it's working so well for me. Not every day is perfect. But compared to the constant pain of Crohn's Disease that I experienced before the diet, a "yucky gut day" here and there is nothing. I've been on the SCD since February, 2007 (and off my 6MP medication since March), so that makes 5 months of no grains, sugars, starches, or any other additives and fillers found in most ready-made, store/restaurant-bought foods. I have to say, I'm used to it. The diet feels normal. I made wheat flour, chocolate chip waffles for Stephen and Sophia on Father's Day, and I didn't feel any sense of jealousy or resentment. I ate my own breakfast of homemade yogurt, an SCD apple pancake, and a banana, loving every bite—knowing that it wouldn't make me feel sick.

Recently, I met with a nutritionist about the SCD, to make certain I was getting the right nutrients for myself and the baby. After reviewing my food diary, she agreed that this was a great diet, especially since I'm feeling so good. She said that the almond flour baked goods have a similar makeup to regular wheat flour baked goods, in terms of vitamins, fiber, protein, and calories. "More veggies," was her only admonition. I already knew that. I'm trying!

The oddest thing about this pregnancy is that since my initial puke-fest on the eve before I found out the good news, I haven't felt nauseated much at all. With my first pregnancy, I was "green" for the whole first trimester. I would gag every time I went to the grocery store, with all those foody smells magnified about 5 billion percent. I feel very fortunate that this time my first trimester was smooth sailing. I've even gained about 8 lbs., which I really needed to do anyway!

A friend who recently had a baby loaned me all her maternity clothes (bless her), and I'm already needing them. I can't believe how fast my belly is pooching out this time around!

SCD Pregnancy Tips   07/13/07

Today, I received an email from a woman who is on the Specific Carbohydrate Diet™ (SCD) after having had a small bowel resection last year. She is now in remission from Crohn's Disease, and although her doctor proclaims it's because of the surgery, she says my story gives her hope that this diet is a key to recovery.

My new SCD friend shared some concerns about pregnancy and Crohn's Disease. I totally know where she's coming from. It's scary to think about starting a family when you don't know if you'll be feeling good or stuck in the ER. Lots to think about.

Four months into my pregnancy, I'm feeling really great. And I have lots of hope that the SCD will get me through any postnatal hormonal fluctuations. My healthcare team has been supportive about my new diet. Here are a few tips for women out there on the SCD who are thinking about getting pregnant:

- SCD-legal prenatal vitamins can be ordered through Kirkman Labs. The product is called Perry Prenatals.
- If your OB wants you to do a screen for diabetes, don't let the lab give you glucose syrup (sugar water). Request to do the blood work 1 hour after a meal instead.
- Consult with a prenatal nutritionist: bring a week-long food diary; a copy of *Breaking The Vicious Cycle;* the label for your prenatal vitamins; and a nutrition breakdown for almond flour, which you can get from www.lucyskitchenshop.com if you ask Lucy for it. My nutritionist helped me make sure I'm getting the right balance for myself and the baby.
- Check with your birthing hospital to see if they can meet your special dietary needs. If not, plan to bring your own food and find out if there is a fridge you can use.
- Something I haven't done yet but plan to do: in the last month before your due date, bake a ton of almond flour goodies (if you can tolerate them) and some SCD-legal meals and freeze them. Then you won't have to stress (as much) when you get home from the hospital.

By the way, it's close to 6 months on the SCD, and I'm still feeling splendid! I've had a cold over the past week and my gut didn't act up at all—I'm usually a mess whenever my immune system kicks in, since it starts to work overtime on my gut too. I think a lot of healing has been taking place.

Happy SCD Anniversary   02/05/08

Today is my one-year anniversary of being on the Specific Carbohydrate Diet™ (SCD) for Crohn's Disease. I guess it's kind of a big day! This morning, while eating some yummy homemade yogurt*, a lemon poppy seed almond-flour muffin (*Turtle Soup,* page 3), and a very ripe banana, I got to thinking about it. A year. A whole YEAR. You know, this diet may end up being the biggest, most important life change I'll ever have made. I am proud of myself for sticking with it—and having had the guts to try it in the first place. Otherwise I'd be sitting here feeling sick, relying on iffy medication, and worrying about the future. But instead, I'm feeling better than I have in my whole life.

On this first anniversary, here are some of the things I'm especially thankful for:

- Great food that makes me feel good.
- Remission without medication.
- My mom Beth, who has been there for me every step of the way.
- My SCD pals who've been a great inspiration. (Thanks for the ice cream maker, Jill!)
- My husband and toddler, for being okay with a slice of bread on the side of an otherwise grain-free meal.
- An amazing pregnancy with no Crohn's complications.
- Feeling well during this hormonally sketchy postpartum time.
- Cassidy, my beautifully healthy SCD baby.

It has been a year of health, happiness, and freedom from gut pain. Here's to feeling good!

---

*Instructions for SCD "legal" yogurt can be found on page 68 of *Turtle Soup.*

SCD and Breastfeeding   11/11/08

Today I got a blog comment from a woman who's interested in trying the Specific Carbohydrate Diet™ (SCD) but has concerns about getting enough calories and nutrients to continue breastfeeding her 8-month-old daughter. Here's her blog comment and my reply, for those who are interested in this topic.

Keep in mind that the food list I included in my reply is enough calories for me when breastfeeding only FOUR times a day with Cassidy eating a lot of solids too. When I was nursing Cassidy 8-10 times a day I ate more almond flour baked goods, probably 2 more muffins or what-have-you per day.

****

Hi Amy,

Just found your blog on a search of "scd diet + breastfeeding" on Google. I'm inspired by your story. I have ulcerative colitis and have been flaring on and off since I was diagnosed 1½ years ago. I flared throughout my pregnancy, was hospitalized for a week, and then gave birth 7 weeks early after a placental abruption. Anyway, my daughter is 8 months old and healthy as can be, but I am still flaring. I'm thinking of trying the SCD, but not sure I'll get all the calories/nutrients required to keep breastfeeding. Are you still breastfeeding Cassidy? Had you talked to your doctors about this at all? Thanks for any help you could offer. Sincerely, Audra

Hi Audra,

I'm sorry to hear about the health issues you've been having. I know how hard it can be to feel sick while taking care of a baby. I hope that I can give you some answers from my journey with the SCD to help you decide if you want to try it. First off, I am still breastfeeding Cassidy four times a day, and I'm, for the most part, feeling great on the diet. I did have a flare several months ago when I cut down on feedings. I think this flare-up was related to hormone fluctuations. So I went back to the intro. diet from *Breaking The Vicious Cycle* (BTVC), and stayed on that for a few weeks. That got me back to a healthy place, and I've been feeling great since. I spoke with a nutritionist when I was pregnant, and she agreed that the SCD is very healthy as long as one includes enough fruits and veggies. She also said the homemade yogurt (I make it from whole milk) and the almond flour baked goods are a great source of calcium, calories, and vitamins. I also take a prenatal vitamin, calcium citrate, and Omega 3-6-9.

My doctors are all thrilled with how I'm doing and say that I'm eating healthier than most of their patients who eat a "normal" diet. I've had no trouble keeping enough weight on and actually am up about 5 lbs. over my pre-SCD weight. You may lose a little weight at first with the intro diet, but once your body gets adjusted and you figure out how many calories from foods other than bread products you need to eat during the day, it should get better. Here's what I ate today as an example of what you might need to eat in order to get enough calories to breastfeed and keep your weight up (I won't include water in my list, but I do drink a lot of it all throughout the day).

breakfast:

      2 eggs

      1 cup homemade whole milk SCD "legal"* yogurt mixed with...

      ½ cup frozen wild blueberries (unsweetened)

      8 oz. apple cider (unsweetened)

snack:

      banana with natural *(100% peanut)* peanut butter

lunch:

      2 slices of "Lois Lang's Luscious Bread" (BTVC, page 127) with butter & honey

      1 oz. SCD "legal"** cheese

      1-2 cups "Creamy Tomato Soup" *(Turtle Soup,* page 29*)*

      handful of baby carrots

      sliced orange

snack:

      cashews and raisins

dinner:

      "Crispy Sautéed Chicken Breasts" *(Turtle Soup,* page 39*)*

      "Roasted Butternut Squash Casserole" *(Turtle Soup,* page 35*)*

      asparagus sautéed in olive oil

      "Applesauce" *(Turtle Soup,* page 13*)*

snack:

      "Peanut Butter Brownies," *(Turtle Soup,* page 50*)*

      ½ cup homemade SCD "legal"* yogurt

Let me know if you have any other questions about anything at all. Starting the SCD is a really big deal and it helps to have a support system, whether it be family, friends, or Internet buddies like me. ☺ Amy

*Instructions for SCD "legal" yogurt can be found on page 68 of *Turtle Soup.*

**For a list of legal and illegal foods for the Specific Carbohydrate Diet™, see: *Breaking the Vicious Cycle: Intestinal Health through Diet, p.p.73-8,* or visit: http://www.breakingtheviciouscycle.info/legal/legal_illegal_a-c.htm

appendix 2: resources for the specific carbohydrate diet™

books

Gottschall, Elaine. *Breaking the Vicious Cycle: Intestinal Health through Diet.* Baltimore, Ontario: Kirkton Press, 2004.*

websites

bethsblog - www.bethsblog.typepad.com

Breaking the Vicious Cycle** - www.breakingtheviciouscycle

Comfy Belly - www.comfybelly.com

The Dietary Adventures of Jill Luck - www.scdadventures.blogspot.com

Kids and SCD - www.pecanbread.com

Kat's Food Blog - http://www.scdkat.com

Lucy's Kitchen Shop*** - www.lucyskitchenshop.com

Mrs. Eds Research and Recipes - http://mrsedsresearchandrecipes.blogspot.com

The SCD Girl - www.scdgirl.blogspot.com

SCD Recipe: Recipes for the Specific Carbohydrate Diet - www.scdrecipe.com

*Elaine Gottschall is the creator of the Specific Carbohydrate Diet™; her book is the SCD "bible."

**For a comprehensive list of SCD "legal" foods please visit:
http://www.breakingtheviciouscycle.info/legal/legal_illegal_a-c.htm
or refer to Elaine Gottshcall's book, *Breaking the Vicious Cycle*.

***Lucy's Kitchen Shop is a supplier of blanched almond flour, yogurt makers, and books for the SCD.

appendix 3 - how to make SCD "legal" yogurt

A delicious mainstay of the Specific Carbohydrate Diet™, yogurt *must* be homemade. Most commercially prepared yogurts contain sugars and starches, and *none* have been sufficiently cultured to eliminate lactose, a milk sugar that's not well tolerated by those with IBS and other bowel diseases. The only way to assure that yogurt is virtually lactose-free is to allow it to culture for 24 hours—thus, the necessity of it being homemade…

You'll need:
    2 quarts fresh milk—low fat or whole*
    a large, heavy saucepan
    a wire whisk
    a 2-quart electric yogurt maker (I use a Yógourmet**)
    2 5g. pkgs. Yógourmet Freeze-Dried Yogurt Starter**

Step 1: *Allow about 20-30 minutes.*

Pour the milk into the heavy saucepan. Place it over medium heat, uncovered. After 5 minutes, vigorously whisk the milk until frothy on top. Continue whisking/frothing the milk every 5 minutes until it comes to a simmer. (Watch the milk carefully as it gets close to the boil—it may boil over.) Take the pan off the heat.

Step 2: *Allow 10-20 minutes.*

Place the pan in the kitchen sink; then fill the sink with cold water, just to the level of the milk, taking care not to splash water into the milk. Set a timer for 10 minutes and let the milk stand; then stir the milk and check its temperature, dripping a little milk off the spoon onto your wrist. It should be tepid, just a little warm to the touch, not at all hot (44-45° C., 111-113° F. on a kitchen thermometer) or you will kill the yogurt culture when doing Step 3. If the milk is too hot, check it again after 5 or 10 minutes.

Step 3: *Allow at least 24 hours.*

Remove the pan from the sink. Dry off the bottom, and place it on your countertop. Sprinkle the starter over the milk, and *immediately* begin whisking it vigorously—whisk for 1 full minute. Pour the milk into the 2-quart inner container that came with your yogurt maker. Cover the container and make sure the lid is *securely* attached. Fill the electric unit with tap water up to the mark on the inside of the reservoir. Place the container holding the milk into the electric unit. The container will float a bit in the water. Cover the unit and plug it in. Let the yogurt "cook" for at least 24 hours. Refrigerate the yogurt for several hours before serving. Whisk the yogurt if you want it to be extra smooth.

*To make "SCD French Cream," a delicious "legal" substitute for sour cream, make yogurt using 2 cups heavy or whipping cream (make sure it's free of thickeners or gums) to 2.5 g. (½ pkg.) Yógourmet Freeze-Dried Yogurt Starter. "French Cream," can be whipped, to taste, with up to ½ cup honey and used as a topping for "Pumpkin Pie," page 52, or fresh fruit. It will keep in the refrigerator for up to 3 days.

**Yogurt makers and starter can be purchased at Lucy's Kitchen Shop (www.lucyskitchenshop.com). You can also get Yógourmet Freeze-Dried Yogurt Starter at some health food stores.

index

 **notes**

✸ notes ✸

✺ notes ✺

notes

☀ **notes** ☀

16824990R00045

Made in the USA
Lexington, KY
13 August 2012